OCS Study MMS 2006-033

FINAL TASK 1 REPORT

VOLUME I

Alternative Oil Spill Occurrence Estimators and their Variability for the Chukchi Sea – Fault Tree Method

MMS Contract Number 1435-01-05-CT-39348

October, 2006

By

BERCHA GROUP

Bercha International Inc.
Calgary, Alberta, Canada

MMS U.S. Department of the Interior
Minerals Management Service
Alaska Outer Continental Shelf Region

OCS Study MMS 2006-033

FINAL TASK 1 REPORT

VOLUME I

Alternative Oil Spill Occurrence Estimators and their Variability for the Chukchi Sea – Fault Tree Method

October, 2006

Principal Investigator: Dr. Frank G. Bercha, P.Eng.

BERCHA GROUP

Bercha International Inc.
2926 Parkdale Boulevard N.W.
Calgary, Alberta, T2N 3S9, Canada
Email: berchaf@berchagroup.com

This study was funded by the U.S. Department of the Interior, Minerals Management Service (MMS), Alaska Outer Continental Shelf Region, Anchorage, under Contract No. 1435-01-05-CT-39348, as part of the MMS Alaska Environmental Studies Program.

ABSTRACT

Oil spill occurrence estimates were generated for several estimated future oil and gas development scenarios (including exploration, production, and abandonment) in the Chukchi Sea Outer Continental Shelf (OCS) lease sale region. Because sufficient historical data on offshore oil spills for this region do not exist, an oil spill occurrence model based on fault tree methodology was developed and applied. Using the fault trees, base data from the Gulf of Mexico including the variability of the data, were modified and augmented to represent expected Arctic offshore oil spillage frequencies. Three principal spill occurrence indicators, as follows, were quantified for each year of each scenario, as well as scenario life of field averages:

- Spill frequency
- Spill frequency per barrel produced
- Spill index, the product of spill size and spill frequency

These indicators were quantified for the following spill sizes:

- Small (S): 50 - 99 bbl
- Medium (M): 100 - 999 bbl
- Large (L): 1,000 - 9,999 bbl
- Huge (H): >= 10,000 bbl
- Significant (SG): >=1,000 bbl

Quantification was carried out for each future year for one principal Chukchi Sea development scenario, with a range of development parameters, in duration up to 36 years. In addition, a comparative scenario for non-Arctic locations was formulated and analyzed for oil spill occurrence. Generally, it was found that the non-Arctic spill indicators were likely to be significantly higher than those for similar scenarios in the Arctic. The computations were carried out using a Monte Carlo process to permit the inclusion of estimated uncertainties in the base and scenario data and Arctic effects. A wide range of details for each scenario was generated, including the following:

- Expected time history of spill occurrences over the scenario life.
- Spill occurrence variations by spill volumes in the above spill size ranges.
- Spill occurrence variation by spill cause such as boat anchoring or ice gouging.
- Spill occurrence contribution from each main facility type, including pipelines, platforms, and wells.
- Comparison of spill occurrence predictions between Arctic and non-Arctic scenarios.
- Life of field averages of spill occurrence estimators.
- The variability in the results due to uncertainties in the inputs was expressed as cumulative distribution functions and statistical measures.

In the final report, a detailed description of the methodology, results, and conclusions and recommendations is given, as well as a section on limitations of the study.

ACKNOWLEDGEMENTS

Grateful acknowledgement for funding and direction is made to MMS Alaska OCS Region. In particular, the following MMS personnel are acknowledged together with their roles:

- Dr. Dick Prentki, Contracting Officer's Technical Representative
- Jim Craig, Resource Evaluation Section
- Caryn Smith, Oil-Spill-Risk-Analysis Coordinator
- Cheryl Anderson, MMS Spill Database Coordinator
- Sharon Teger, Contracting Officer
- Warren Horowitz, Oceanographer
- Dennis Hinnah, Office of Field Operations

This work was carried out by Bercha International Inc. Key Bercha personnel on the project team were as follows:

- Dr. Frank G. Bercha, Project Manager and Principal Engineer
- Milan Cerovšek, Reliability Engineering Specialist
- Edmund A. Yasinko, Offshore Pipeline Specialist
- Wesley Abel, Offshore Engineering Specialist
- Susan Charlton, Editorial and Word Processing Manager

EXECUTIVE SUMMARY

A. Summary of Work Done

Oil spill occurrence estimators were generated for several estimated future oil and gas development scenarios (including exploration, production, and abandonment) in the Chukchi Sea Outer Continental Shelf (OCS) lease sale region. Because sufficient historical data on offshore oil spills for these regions do not exist, an oil spill occurrence model based on fault tree methodology was developed and applied. Using the fault trees, base data from the Gulf of Mexico, including their variability, were modified and augmented to represent expected Arctic offshore oil spillage frequencies for the Chukchi Sea region under study. Three principal spill occurrence indicators, as follows, were quantified for each year of each scenario, as well as scenario life of field averages:

- Spill frequency
- Spill frequency per barrel produced
- Spill index, the product of spill size and spill frequency

These indicators were quantified for the following spill sizes:

- Small (S): 50 - 99 bbl
- Medium (M): 100 - 999 bbl
- Large (L): 1,000 - 9,999 bbl
- Huge (H): >=10,000 bbl
- Signficant (SG): >=1,000 bbl

Fractional spill sizes were rounded up or down to the nearest whole number, with rounding up for any decimal ending in 5.

Quantification was carried out for each future year for an estimated Chukchi Sea exploration and development scenario, extending 36 years from 2009 to 2044 In addition, a comparative scenario for non-Arctic locations was formulated and analyzed for oil spill occurrence. Generally, it was found that the non-Arctic spill indicators were likely to be higher than those for a similar scenario in the Arctic. The computations were carried out using a Monte Carlo process to permit the inclusion of estimated uncertainties in the input data. A wide range of details for each scenario was generated, including the following:

- Expected time history of spill occurrences over the scenario life.
- Spill occurrence variations by spill volumes in the above spill size ranges.
- Spill occurrence variation by spill cause such as boat anchoring or ice gouging.

- Spill occurrence contribution from each main facility type, including pipelines, platforms, and wells.
- Comparison of spill occurrence predictions between Arctic and non-Arctic scenarios.
- The variability in the results due to uncertainties in the input data expressed as cumulative distribution functions and statistical measures.

In the final report, a detailed description of the methodology, results, and conclusions and recommendations is given, as well as a section on limitations of the study.

B. Conclusions

B.1 General Conclusions

Oil spill occurrence indicators were quantified for future offshore development scenarios in the Chukchi Sea Sale 193 area. The quantification considered variability of historical and future scenario data, as well as that of Arctic effects to predict oil spill occurrence indicators. Consideration of the variability of all input data yields both higher variability and a higher expected value of the spill occurrence indicators. The three types of spill occurrence indicators were: annual oil spill frequency, annual oil spill frequency per barrel produced, and annual spill index – and, additionally, the life of field averages for each of these three oil spill indicators were assessed.

B.2 Oil Spill Occurrence Indicators by Spill Size

How do spill indicators for the different scenarios and for their non-Arctic counterparts vary by spill size and source? Table 1 summarizes the Life of Field (LOF) average spill indicator values. Figure 1 illustrates these. The following can be observed from Table 1.

- Spill frequency per year and per barrel-year decreases significantly with increasing spill size for all scenarios.
- The spill index increases significantly with spill size for both scenarios.
- All non-Arctic scenario spill indicators are greater than their Arctic counterparts. Non-Arctic spill indicators are approximately 30% greater.

Table 1
Summary of Life of Field Average Spill Indicators by Spill Source and Size

Spill Indicators LOF Average	Chukchi Sea			Chukchi Sea - Non Arctic		
	Spill Frequency per 10^3 years	Spill Frequency per 10^9 bbl produced	Spill Index [bbl]	Spill Frequency per 10^3 years	Spill Frequency per 10^9 bbl produced	Spill Index [bbl]
Small and Medium Spills 50-999 bbl	18.750	0.675	8	26.111	0.940	11
	57%	**57%**	**2%**	**53%**	**53%**	**2%**
Large Spills 1000-9999 bbl	8.735	0.314	58	14.808	0.533	95
	26%	**26%**	**13%**	**30%**	**30%**	**14%**
Huge Spills =>10000 bbl	5.578	0.201	399	8.593	0.309	574
	17%	**17%**	**86%**	**17%**	**17%**	**84%**
Significant Spills =>1000 bbl	14.313	0.515	458	23.401	0.842	669
	43%	**43%**	**98%**	**47%**	**47%**	**98%**
All Spills	33.063	1.190	465	49.512	1.782	680
	100%	**100%**	**100%**	**100%**	**100%**	**100%**
Pipeline Spills	20.301	0.730	69	33.248	1.196	125
	61%	**61%**	**15%**	**67%**	**67%**	**18%**
Platform Spills	7.362	0.265	9	8.668	0.312	10
	22%	**22%**	**2%**	**18%**	**18%**	**2%**
Well Spills	5.401	0.194	387	7.595	0.273	544
	16%	**16%**	**83%**	**15%**	**15%**	**80%**
Platform and Well Spills	12.763	0.459	396	16.264	0.585	554
	39%	**39%**	**85%**	**33%**	**33%**	**82%**
All Spills	33.063	1.190	465	49.512	1.782	680
	100%	**100%**	**100%**	**100%**	**100%**	**100%**

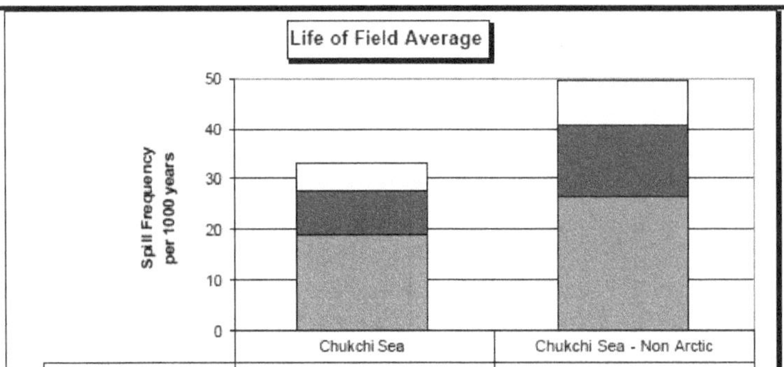

	Chukchi Sea	Chukchi Sea - Non Arctic
Huge Spills =>10000 bbl	5.578	8.593
Large Spills 1000-9999 bbl	8.735	14 808
Small and Medium Spills 50-999 bbl	18.750	26.111

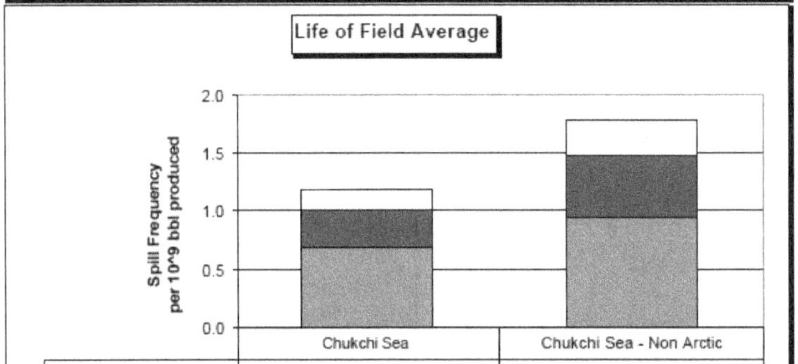

	Chukchi Sea	Chukchi Sea - Non Arctic
Huge Spills =>10000 bbl	0.201	0.309
Large Spills 1000-9999 bbl	0.314	0.533
Small and Medium Spills 50-999 bbl	0.675	0.940

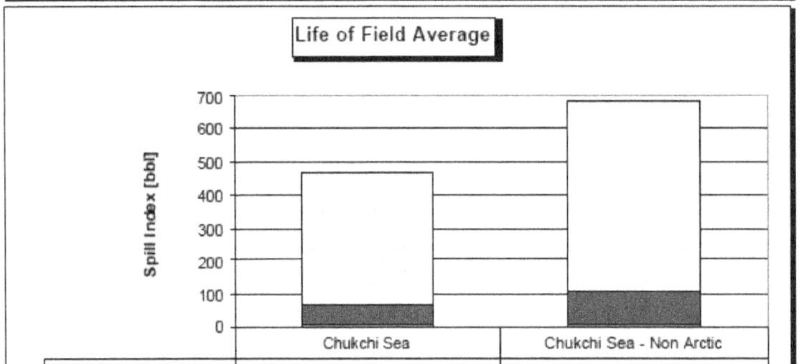

	Chukchi Sea	Chukchi Sea - Non Arctic
Huge Spills =>10000 bbl	399	574
Large Spills 1000-9999 bbl	58	95
Small and Medium Spills 50-999 bbl	8	11

Figure 1
Life of Field Spill Indicators – By Spill Size

B.3 Oil Spill Occurrence Indicators by Spill Source

How do the spill indicators vary by spill source facility type for representative scenarios? The contributions of spill indicators by source facility have been summarized by life of field averages, in Table 1 and also in Figure 2, for all spill sizes. Table 1 and Figure 2 give the component contributions, in absolute value and percent, for each of the main facility types; namely, pipelines (P/L), platforms, and wells. The following may be noted from Table 1:

- Pipelines contribute the most (61%) to the two spill frequency indicators.
- Platforms are next in relative contribution to spill frequencies (22%) and least in contribution to spill index (2%).
- Wells are by far (at 83%) the highest contributors to spill index, while platforms and wells together are responsible for a 82% contribution to the spill index.
- It can be concluded that pipelines are likely to have the most, but smaller spills, while wells will have the least number, but largest spills. Platforms will be in between, with a tendency towards more spills than wells, but less or about the same number as platforms.

Figures 3 and 4 show relative contributions by facility and spill size to the maximum production year 2024 and Life of Field average spill indicators, respectively. Although Life of Field average spill indicator absolute values are significantly smaller than the maximum production year values, the proportional contributions by spill facility source and spill size are almost identical.

B.4 Variability of Oil Spill Occurrence Indicators

Figures 5, 6, and 7 show the Cumulative Distribution Functions for each of the Chukchi Sea Life ofField average spill indicators by spill size and source. Generally, the following can be observed from the figures:

- The variance of the frequency spill indicators (Figures 5 and 6) decreases as spill size increases for pipelines and platforms. In other words, small and medium spills illustrate the largest variability; huge spills show the least variability for these facilities.
- The opposite occurs for wells.
- The variability of the spill index (Figure 7) shows the opposite trend for pipelines and platforms.

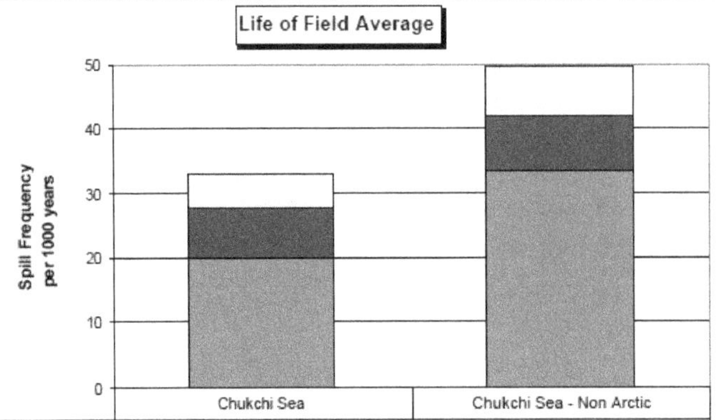

	Chukchi Sea	Chukchi Sea - Non Arctic
Well Spills	5.401	7 595
Platform Spills	7 362	8 668
Pipeline Spills	20.301	33.248

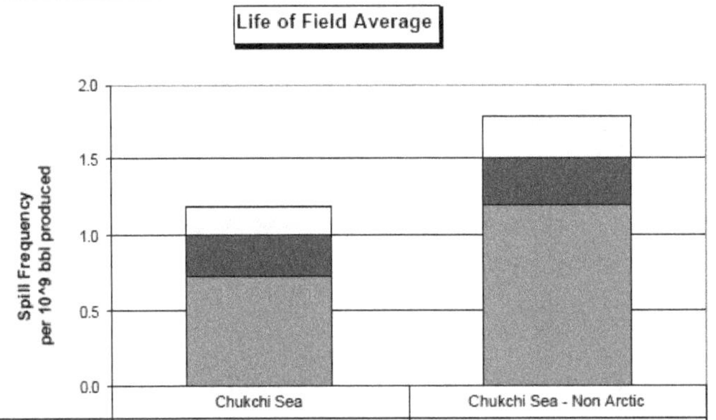

	Chukchi Sea	Chukchi Sea - Non Arctic
Well Spills	0.194	0.273
Platform Spills	0.265	0.312
Pipeline Spills	0.730	1.196

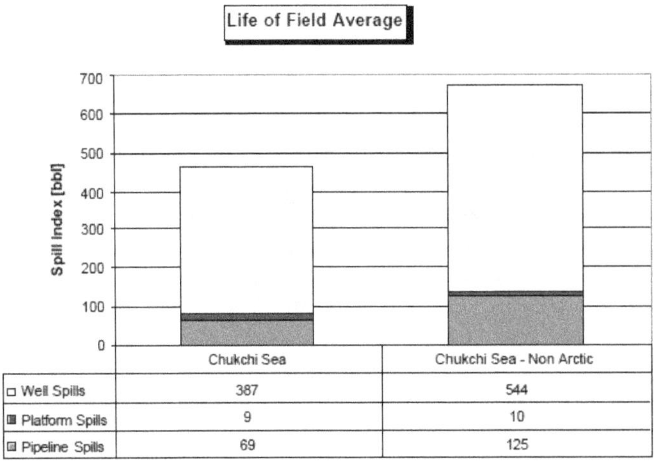

	Chukchi Sea	Chukchi Sea - Non Arctic
Well Spills	387	544
Platform Spills	9	10
Pipeline Spills	69	125

Figure 2
Life of Field Spill Indicators – By Source Composition

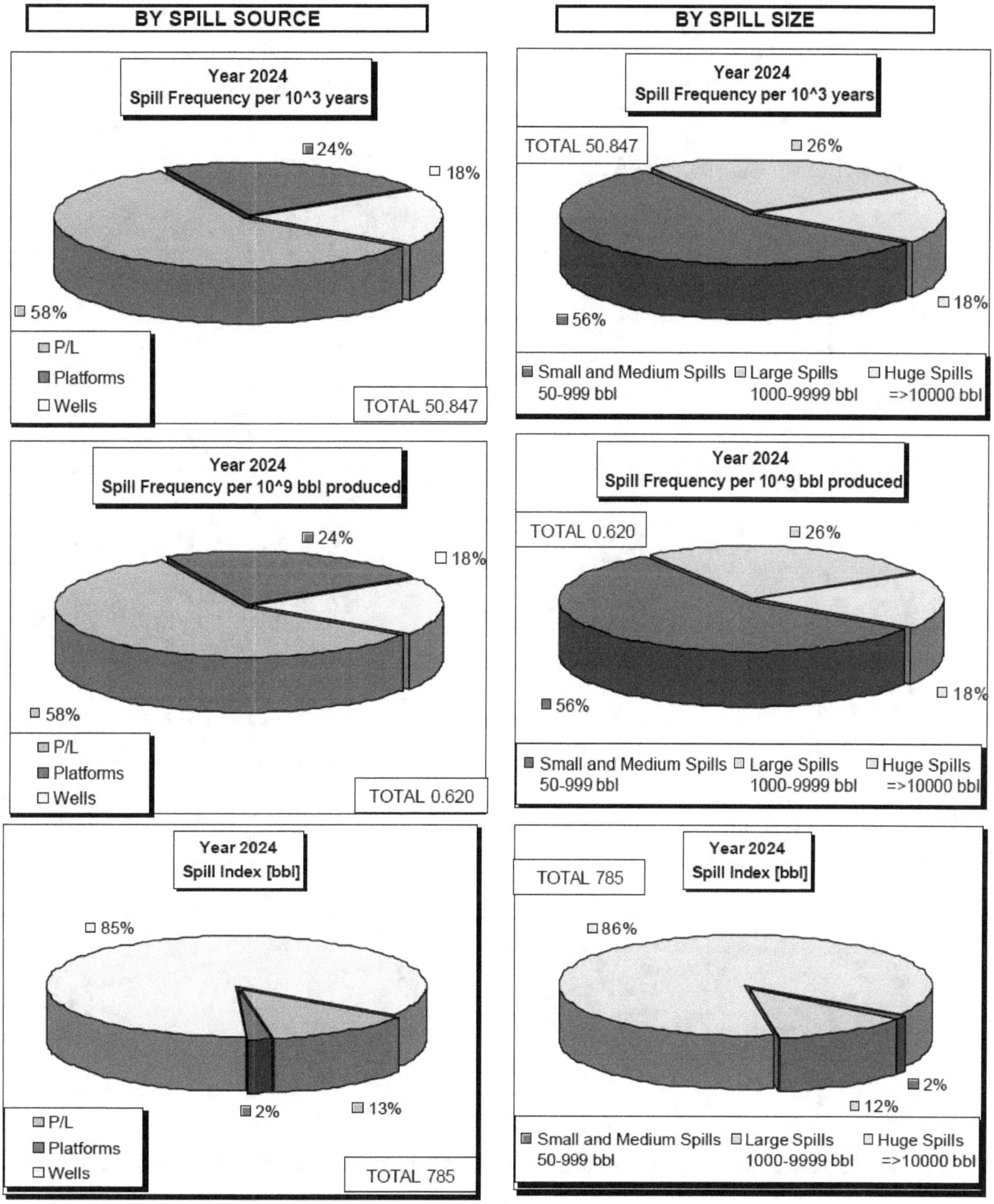
BY SPILL SOURCE
BY SPILL SIZE
Year 2024
Spill Frequency per 10^3 years
24%
18%
58%
P/L
Platforms
Wells
TOTAL 50.847
Year 2024
Spill Frequency per 10^3 years
TOTAL 50.847
26%
56%
18%
Small and Medium Spills 50-999 bbl
Large Spills 1000-9999 bbl
Huge Spills =>10000 bbl
Year 2024
Spill Frequency per 10^9 bbl produced
24%
18%
58%
P/L
Platforms
Wells
TOTAL 0.620
Year 2024
Spill Frequency per 10^9 bbl produced
TOTAL 0.620
26%
56%
18%
Small and Medium Spills 50-999 bbl
Large Spills 1000-9999 bbl
Huge Spills =>10000 bbl
Year 2024
Spill Index [bbl]
85%
2%
13%
P/L
Platforms
Wells
TOTAL 785
Year 2024
Spill Index [bbl]
TOTAL 785
86%
2%
12%
Small and Medium Spills 50-999 bbl
Large Spills 1000-9999 bbl
Huge Spills =>10000 bbl

Figure 3
Chukchi Sea – Year 2024 – Spill Indicator Composition by Source and Spill Size

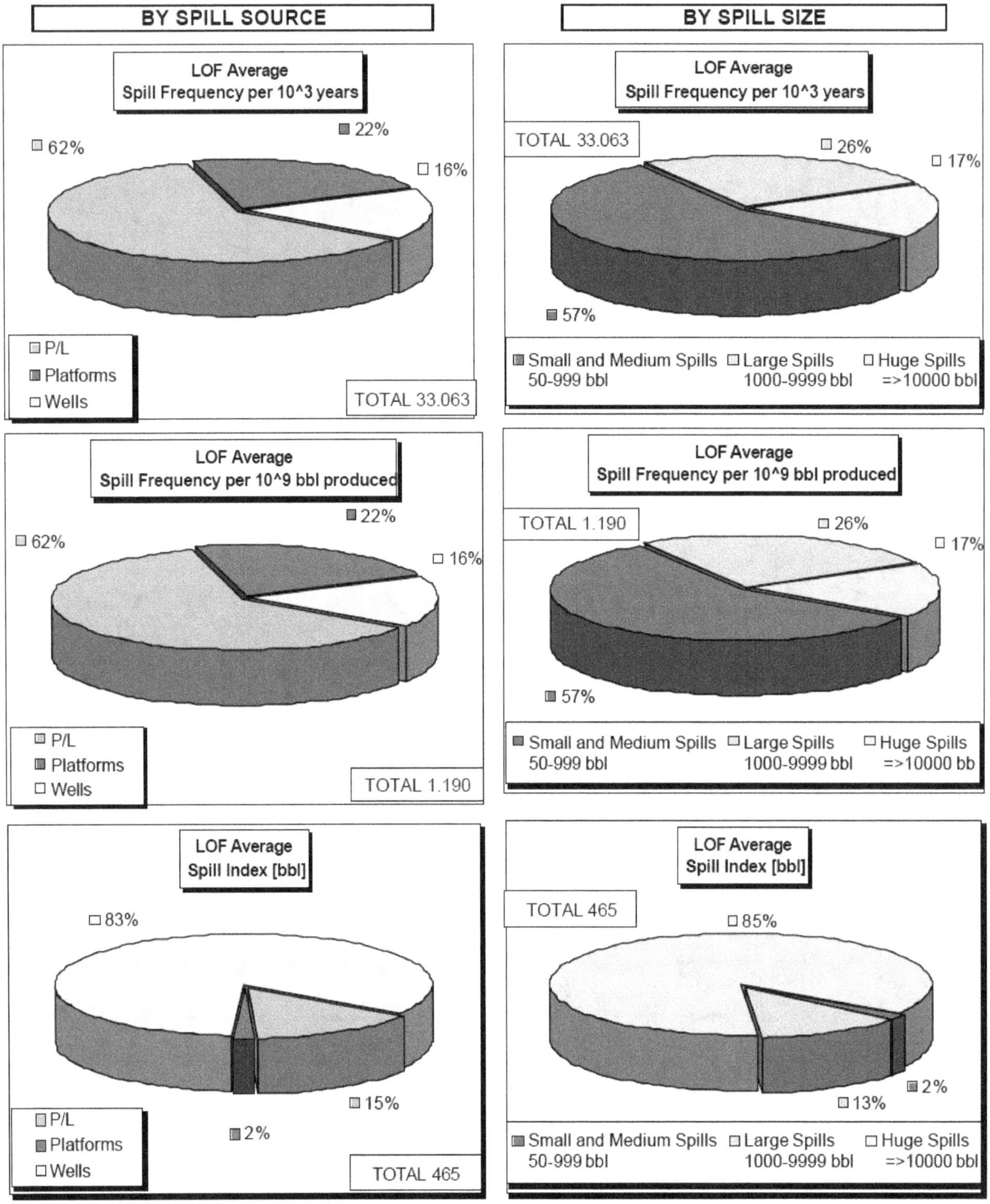
BY SPILL SOURCE
BY SPILL SIZE
LOF Average
Spill Frequency per 10^3 years
62%
22%
16%
P/L
Platforms
Wells
TOTAL 33.063
LOF Average
Spill Frequency per 10^3 years
TOTAL 33.063
26%
17%
57%
Small and Medium Spills 50-999 bbl
Large Spills 1000-9999 bbl
Huge Spills =>10000 bbl
LOF Average
Spill Frequency per 10^9 bbl produced
62%
22%
16%
P/L
Platforms
Wells
TOTAL 1.190
LOF Average
Spill Frequency per 10^9 bbl produced
TOTAL 1.190
26%
17%
57%
Small and Medium Spills 50-999 bbl
Large Spills 1000-9999 bbl
Huge Spills =>10000 bb
LOF Average
Spill Index [bbl]
83%
15%
2%
P/L
Platforms
Wells
TOTAL 465
LOF Average
Spill Index [bbl]
TOTAL 465
85%
13%
2%
Small and Medium Spills 50-999 bbl
Large Spills 1000-9999 bbl
Huge Spills =>10000 bbl

Figure 4
Chukchi Sea – Life of Field Average Spill Indicator Composition by Source and Spill Size

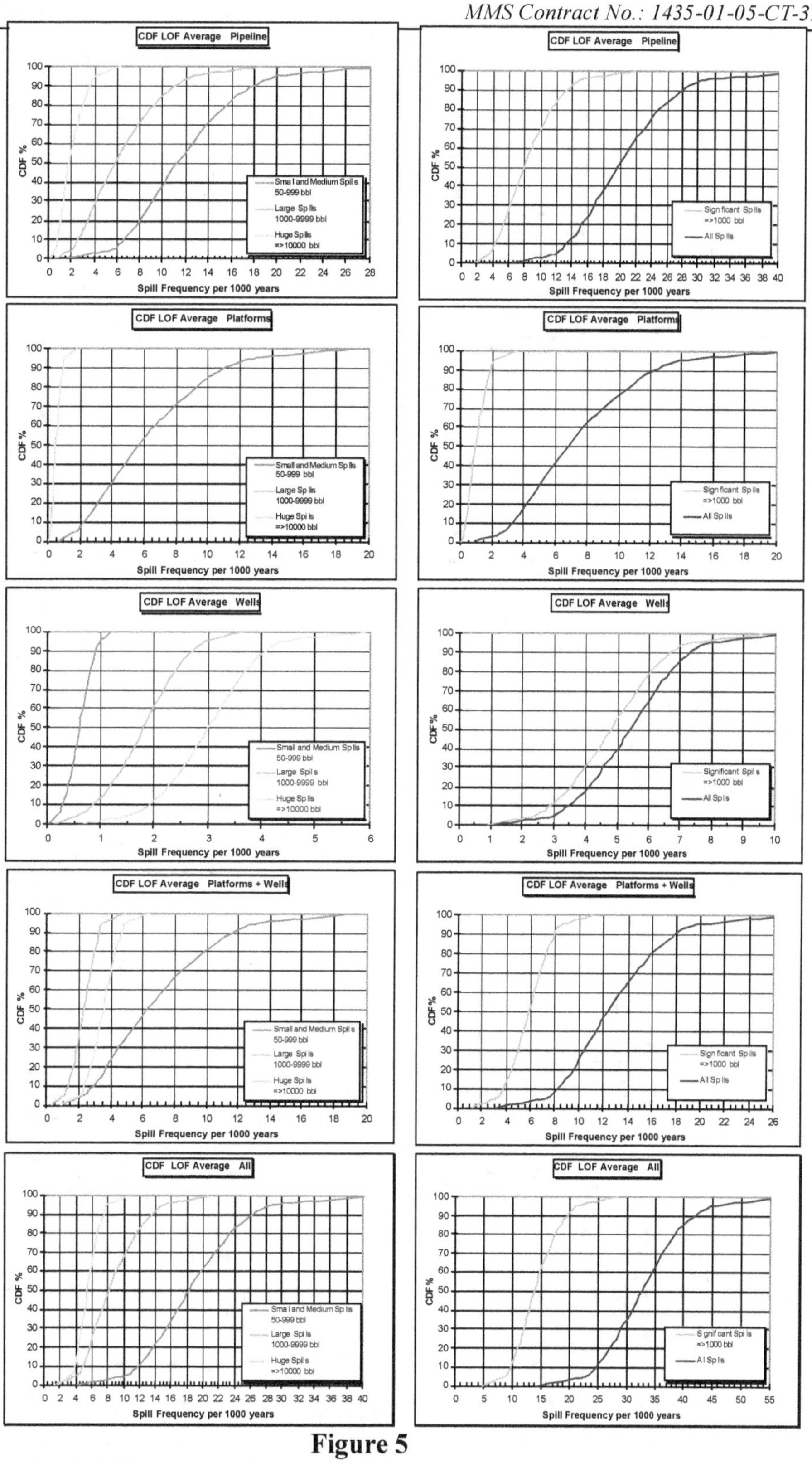

Figure 5
Chukchi Sea Life of Field Average Spill Frequency – CDF

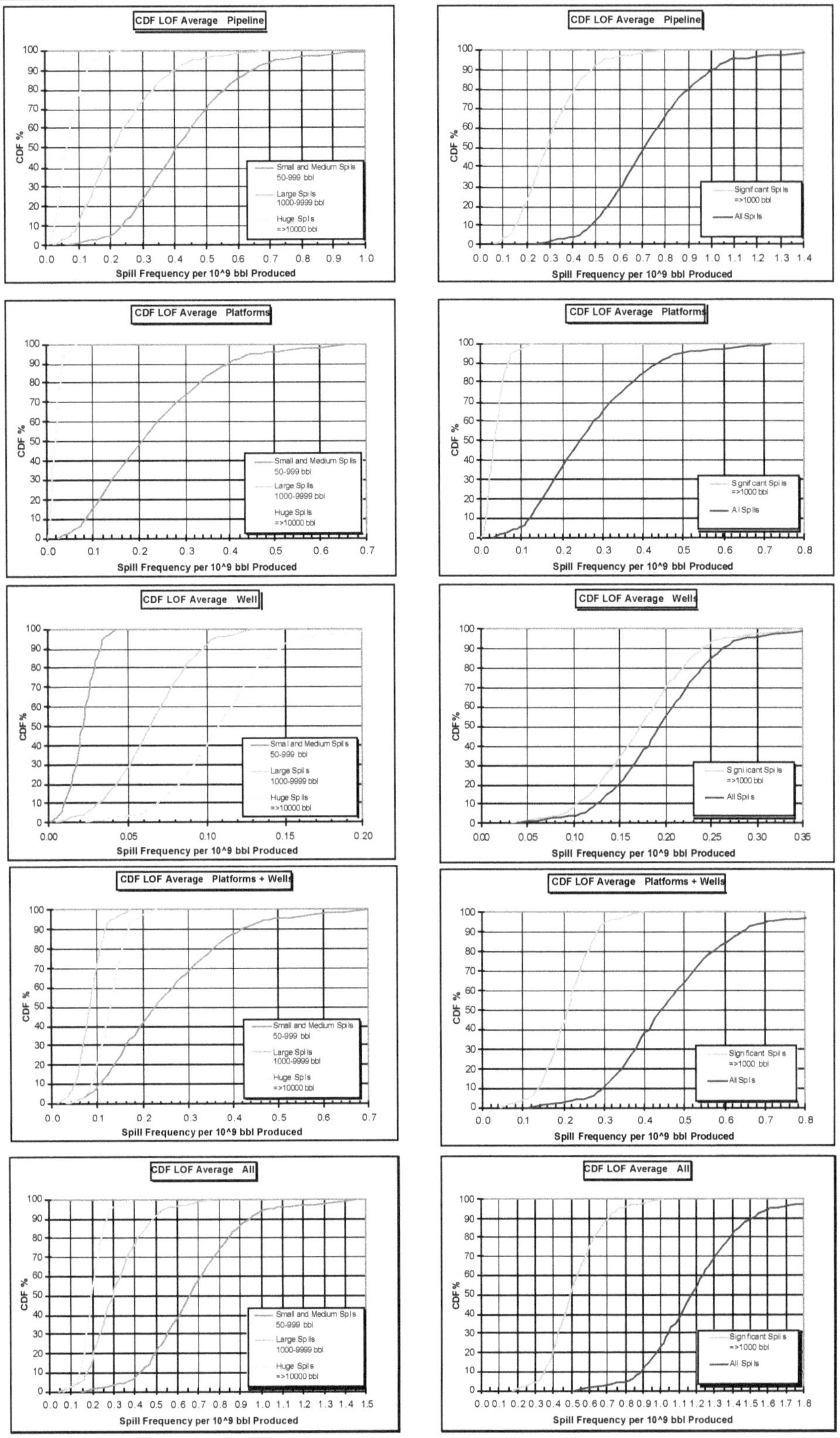

Figure 6
Chukchi Sea Life of Field Average Spill Frequency per Barrel Produced – CDF

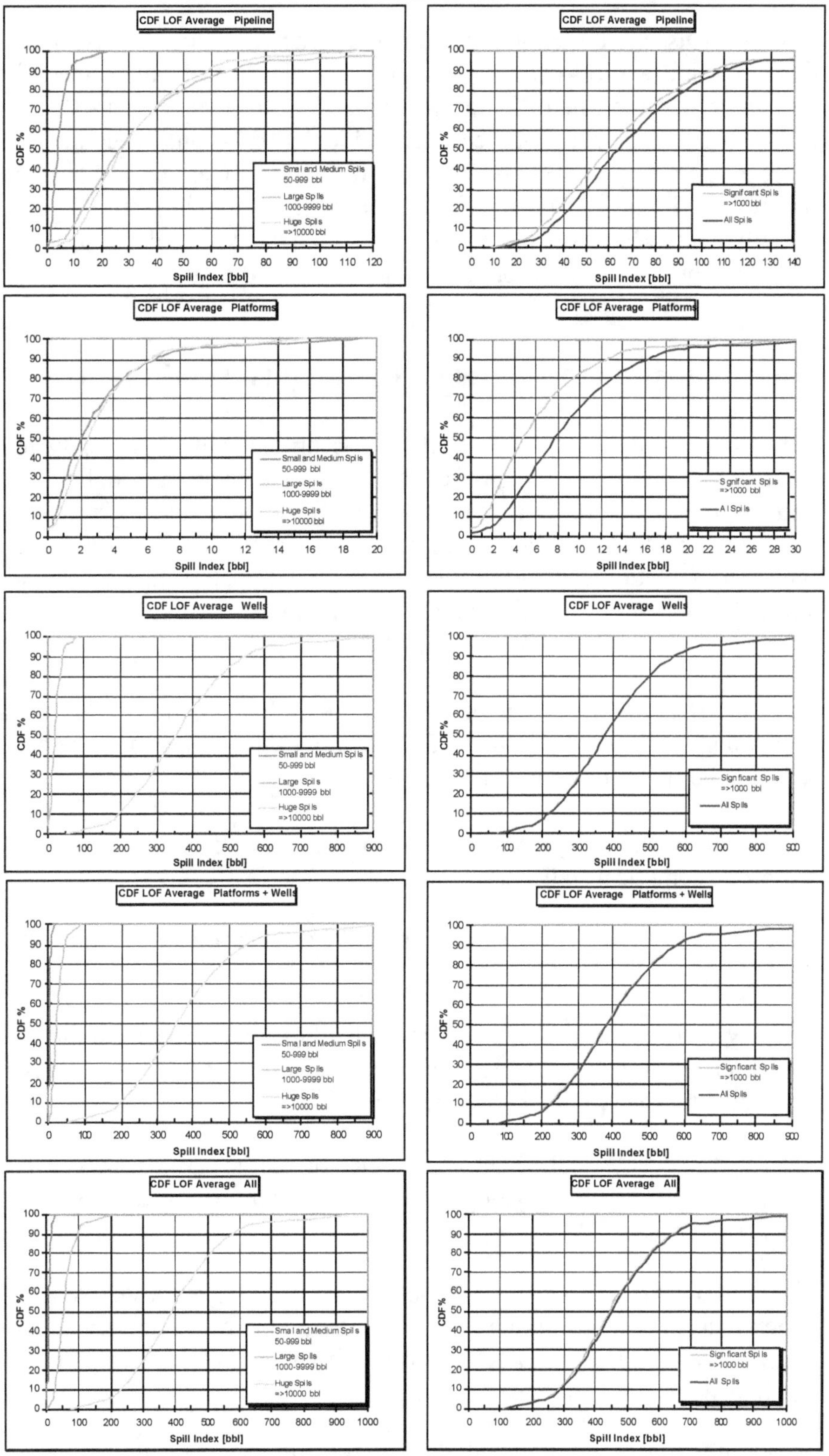

Figure 7
Chukchi Sea Life of Field Average Spill Index (bbl) – CDF

The Cumulative Distribution Functions contain extensive information on the statistical properties of the spill indicators. For example, from Figure 5, it can be seen, for all significant spills, that the Life of Field average mean (50%) value of 14 (spills per 1,000 years) ranges between 23 and 7 at the upper and lower 95% confidence intervals. A similar percentage variation is shown for the Life of Field average spill frequency per barrel produced in Figure 6. The spill index variability shown in Figure 7 is proportionally higher. For example, in Figure 7, the mean value of the significant spills index of 450 per billion barrels produced ranges from 250 to 700.

C. Conclusions on the Methodology and its Applicability

An analytical tool for the prediction of oil spill occurrence indicators for systems without history, such as future offshore oil production developments in the Chukchi Sea, has been developed based on the utilization of fault tree methodology. Although the results generated are voluminous, they are essentially transparent, simple, and easy to understand. The analytical tool developed is also quite transparent, very efficient in terms of computer time and input-output capability. In addition, the predictive model is setup so that any input variables can be entered as distributions.

A wealth of information that can be utilized for the optimal planning and regulation of future developments is generated by the analytical tool. Key aspects of the analytical tool capability may be summarized as follows:

- Ability to generate expected and mean values as well as their variability in rigorous numerical statistical format.
- Use of verifiable input data based on MMS or other historical spill data and statistics.
- Ability to independently vary the impacts of different causes on the spill occurrences as well as add new causes such as some of those that may be expected for the Arctic or other new environments.
- Ability to generate spill occurrence indicator characteristics such as annual variations, facility contributions, spill size distributions, and life of field (Life of Field) averages.
- Ability to generate comparative spill occurrence indicators such as those of comparable scenarios in more temperate regions. The model developed provides a basis for estimating each Arctic effect's importance through sensitivity analysis as well as propagation of uncertainties.
- Capability to quantify uncertainties rigorously, together with their measures of variability.

D. Limitations of the Methodology and Results

During the work, a number of limitations in the input data, the scenarios, the application of the fault tree methodology, and finally the oil spill occurrence indicators themselves have been identified. These shortcomings are summarized in the following paragraphs.

Two categories of input data were used; namely the historical spill data and the Arctic effect data. Although a verifiable and optimal historical spill data set has been used, the following shortcomings may be noted:

- Gulf of Mexico (OCS) historical data bases were provided by MMS for pipelines and facilities, and were used as a starting point for the fault tree analysis. Although these data are adequate, a broader population base would give more robust statistics. Unfortunately, data from a broader population base, such as the North Sea, do not contain the level of detail provided in the GOM data.

- The Arctic effects include modifications in causes associated with the historical data set as well as additions of spill causes unique to the Arctic environment. Quantification of existing causes for Arctic effects was done in a relative cursory way restricted to engineering judgment.

- Upheaval buckling effect assessments were included on the basis of an educated guess; no engineering analysis was carried out for the assessment of frequencies to be expected for these effects.

- A reproducible but relatively elementary analysis of gouging and scour effects was carried out.

The scenarios are those developed for use in the MMS Alaska OCS Region Environmental Impact Statements for Oil and Gas Lease Sales. As estimated they appear reasonable and were incorporated in the form provided.

- The only shortcoming appears to be that the facility abandonment rate is significantly lower than the rate of decline in production.

The following comments can be made on limitations associated with the indicators that have been generated:

- The indicators have inherited the deficiencies of the input and scenario data noted above.

- The model generating the indicators is fundamentally a linear model which ignores the effects of scale, of time variations such as the learning and wear-out curves (Bathtub curve), and production volume non-linear effects.

E. Recommendations

The following recommendations based on the work may be made:

- Continue to utilize the Monte Carlo spill occurrence indicator model for new scenarios to support MMS needs, as it is currently the best predictive spill occurrence model available.
- Utilize the oil spill occurrence indicator model to generate additional model validation information, including direct application to specific non-Arctic scenarios, such as GOM projects, which have an oil spill statistical history.
- Utilize the oil spill occurrence indicator model in a sensitivity mode to identify the importance of different Arctic effect variables introduced to provide a prioritized list of those items having the highest potential impact on Arctic oil spills.
- Generalize the model so that it can be run both in an adjusted expected value and a distributed value (Monte Carlo) form with the intent that expected value form can be utilized without the Monte Carlo add-in for preliminary estimates and sensitivity analyses, while for more comprehensive rigorous studies, the Monte Carlo version can be used.

TABLE OF CONTENTS

VOLUME I

CHAPTER **PAGE**

Abstract .... *i*
Acknowledgements .... *ii*
Executive Summary .... *iii*
Table of Contents .... *xvii*
List of Appendices .... *xix*
List of Tables .... *xx*
List of Figures .... *xxi*
Glossary of Terms and Acronyms .... *xxii*

1 Introduction 1.1

1.1 General Introduction 1.1
1.2 Study Objectives 1.1
1.3 Study Area Definition 1.2
1.4 General Background 1.2
1.5 Technical Approaches 1.4
1.6 Scope of Work 1.5
1.7 Work Organization 1.6
1.8 Outline of Report 1.8

2 Historical Data 2.1

2.1 Approaches to Historical Data 2.1
2.2 Pipeline Oil Spill Data 2.1
2.3 Platform Spill Data 2.5
2.4 Oil Well Blowout Data 2.5
2.5 Arctic Effects Historical Data 2.9
2.5.1 General Approaches to the Quantification of Arctic Effects *2.9*
2.5.2 Ice Gouging *2.9*
2.5.3 Strudel Scour *2.10*
2.5.4 Upheaval Buckling *2.12*
2.5.5 Thaw Settlement *2.12*
2.5.6 Platform Arctic Unique Effects *2.12*
2.6 Historical Spill Size Distribution 2.14

3 Future Development Scenarios 3.1

3.1 Approaches to Future Development Scenarios 3.1
3.2 Chukchi Sea Development Scenarios 3.3

4 Fault Tree Analysis for Arctic Oil Spill Frequencies 4.1
4.1 General Description of Fault Tree Analysis 4.1
4.2 Fault Tree Methodology 4.1
4.2.1 Fault Tree Analysis Basics 4.1
4.2.2 Current Application of Fault Trees 4.3
4.2.3 Monte Carlo Simulation 4.5
4.2.4 Distribution Derived from Historical Data for Monte Carlo Analysis 4.7
4.2.5 Approaches to Assessment of Arctic Spill Frequency Variability 4.10
4.3 Pipeline Fault Tree Analysis 4.10
4.3.1 Arctic Pipeline Spill Causal Frequency Distributions 4.10
4.3.3 Arctic Pipeline Fault Tree Frequency Calculations 4.14
4.4 Platform Fault Tree Analysis 4.21
4.4.1 Arctic Platform Spill Causal Frequency Distributions 4.21
4.4.2 Arctic Platform Fault Tree Spill Frequency Calculations 4.21
4.5 Blowout Frequency Analysis 4.28
4.5.1 Well Blowout First Order Arctic Effects 4.28
4.5.2 Arctic Well Blowout Spill Frequency Calculations 4.28
4.6 Spill Volume Distributions 4.28

5 Oil Spill Occurrence Indicator Quantification 5.1
5.1 Definition of Oil Spill Occurrence Indicators 5.1
5.2 Oil Spill Occurrence Indicator Calculation Process 5.1
5.3 Summary of Chukchi Sea Oil Spill Occurrence Indicators 5.3
5.3.1 Chukchi Sea Oil Spill Occurrence Indicators 5.3
5.3.2 Comparative Non-Arctic Indicator Assessment 5.11
5.4 Summary of Representative Oil Spill Occurrence Indicator Results 5.20

6 Conclusions and Recommendations 6.1
6.1 Conclusions 6.1
6.1.1 General Conclusions 6.1
6.1.2 Oil Spill Occurrence Indicators by Spill Size 6.1
6.1.3 Oil Spill Occurrence Indicators by Spill Source 6.4
6.1.4 Variability of Oil Spill Occurrence Indicators 6.4
6.2 Conclusions on the Methodology and Its Applicability 6.5
6.3 Limitations of the Methodology and Results 6.6
6.4 Recommendations 6.7

References R.1

LIST OF APPENDICES

(VOLUME II – APPENDICES)

APPENDIX

1 **Historical Data Analysis**

2 **Fault Tree Analysis**

3 **Hazard Scenarios**

4 **Spill Occurrence**

4.1 Arctic Spill Occurrence – Chukchi Sea

4.2 Arctic Spill Occurrence – Chukchi Sea Non-Arctic

5 **Conclusions**

LIST OF TABLES

TABLE **PAGE**

2.1 GOM OCS Pipeline Spills Statistics Summary (1972-1999) 2.2
2.2 Analysis of GOM OCS Spill Data for Causal Distribution and Spill Size....2.3
2.3 Distribution and Frequency of Historical Spills - Pipeline....2.4
2.4 Pipeline Historical Spill Frequency Variability....2.4
2.5 Analysis of GOM OCS Platform Spill Data for Causal Distribution Spill Size (1972-1999) .2.6
2.6 Causal and Spill Size Distribution of GOM OCS Platform Spills (1972-1999)....2.6
2.7 Platform Historical Spill Frequency Variability....2.6
2.8 Summary of North Sea and Gulf of Mexico Blowout Rates 2.7
2.9 Well Blowout Historical Spill Size Distribution....2.7
2.10 Well Blowout Historical Spill Probability and Size Variability....2.8
2.11 Summary of Pipeline Unique Arctic Effect Inputs....2.11
2.12 Summary of Platform Unique Arctic Effect Inputs....2.13
2.13 Summary of Historical Spill Size Distribution Parameters 2.14

3.1 Classification of Development Scenarios....3.2
3.2 Summary of Exploration and Development Scenario, Chukchi Sea OCS....3.4
3.3 Chukchi Sea Development Data (2009-2044)....3.5
3.4 Chukchi Sea Development Parameter Ranges (2009-2044) 3.8

4.1 Pipeline Spill Frequency Triangular Distribution Properties 4.8
4.2 Platform Spill Frequency Triangular Distribution Properties 4.8
4.3 Well Blowout Spill Frequency Triangular Distribution Properties....4.9
4.4 Pipeline Arctic Effect Derivation Summary....4.11
4.5 Pipeline Arctic Effect Distribution Derivation Summary 4.13
4.6 Arctic Pipeline Small Spill (50-99 bbl) Frequencies....4.16
4.7 Arctic Pipeline Medium Spill (100-999 bbl) Frequencies....4.17
4.8 Arctic Pipeline Large Spill (1,000-9,999 bbl) Frequencies....4.18
4.9 Arctic Pipeline Huge Spill (=10,000 bbl) Frequencies....4.19
4.10 Arctic Pipeline Spill Frequencies Expected Value Summary 4.20
4.11 Platform Arctic Effect Derivation Summary....4.22
4.12 Platform Arctic Effect Distribution Derivation Summary....4.23
4.13 Arctic Platform Small and Medium Spill Frequencies....4.25
4.14 Arctic Platform Large and Huge Spill Frequencies....4.26
4.15 Arctic Platforms Spill Frequency Expected Value Summary 4.27
4.16 Well Fault Tree Analysis Arctic Effect Summary....4.29
4.17 Arctic Well Blowout Frequencies 4.30
4.18 Summary of Spill Size Distribution Parameters....4.31

5.1 Chukchi Sea Year 2024 – Monte Carlo Results 5.9
5.2 Composition of Spill Indicators –Life of Field Average 5.12
5.3 Summary of Life of Field Average Spill Indicators by Spill Source and Size ...5.17

6.1 Summary of Life of Field Average Spill Indicators by Spill Source and Size 6.2

LIST OF FIGURES

FIGURE **PAGE**

1.1 Study Area Map 1.3
1.2 Calculation Flow Chart 1.7

4.1 Fault Tree Basics 4.2
4.2 Example of Fault Tree to Transform Historical (GOM) to Arctic Spill Frequencies 4.4
4.3 Monte Carlo Technique Schematic 4.6
4.4 Large Spill Frequencies for Pipeline 4.15
4.5 Spill Frequencies Platform Fault Tree 4.24

5.1 Calculation Flow Chart 5.2
5.2 Chukchi Sea Spill Frequency per 1,000 Years 5.4
5.3 Chukchi Sea Spill Frequency per 10^9 Barrels Produced 5.4
5.4 Chukchi Sea Spill Index 5.5
5.5 Chukchi Sea Spill Indicators – Pipeline 5.6
5.6 Chukchi Sea Spill Indicators – Platforms 5.7
5.7 Chukchi Sea Spill Indicators – Wells 5.8
5.8 Chukchi Sea Spill Indicator Distributions – Year 2024 .... 5.10
5.9 Chukchi Sea Life of Field Average Spill Frequency 5.13
5.10 Chukchi Sea Life of Field Average Spills per Barrel Produced 5.14
5.11 Chukchi Sea Spill Frequency – Arctic and Non-Arctic 5.15
5.12 Chukchi Sea Spill Frequency per 10^9 Barrels Produced – Arctic and Non-Arctic 5.15
5.13 Chukchi Sea Spill Index – Arctic and Non-Arctic 5.16
5.14 Life of Field Spill Indicators –By Spill Size 5.18
5.15 Life of Field Spill Indicators – By Source Composition 5.19
5.16 Chukchi Sea – Year 2024 – Spill Indicator Composition by Source 5.21
5.17 Chukchi Sea – Life of Field Average Spill Indicator Composition by Source 5.22
5.18 Chukchi Sea Life of Field Average Spill Frequency - CDF 5.24
5.19 Chukchi Sea Life of Field Average Spill Frequency per Barrel Produced – CDF 5.25
5.20 Chukchi Sea Life of Field Average Spill Index (bbl) – CDF 5.30

6.1 Life of Field Spill Indicators – By Spill Size 6.3

GLOSSARY OF TERMS AND ACRONYMS

Bbbl	**B**illion Barrels
CDF	**C**umulative **D**istribution **F**unction
Consequence	The direct effect of an accidental event.
GOM	**G**ulf **o**f **M**exico
Hazard	A condition with a potential to create risks such as accidental leakage of natural gas from a pressurized vessel.
KBpd	Thousand Barrels per day
LOF	**L**ife **o**f **F**ield
MMbbl	Million Barrels
MMS	**M**inerals **M**anagement **S**ervice, Department of the Interior
Monte Carlo	A numerical method for evaluating algebraic combinations of statistical distributions.
OCS	**O**uter **C**ontinental **S**helf
QRA	**Q**uantitative **R**isk **A**ssessment
Risk	A compound measure of the probability and magnitude of adverse effect.
RLS	Release
SINTEF	The Foundation of Scientific and Industrial Research at the Norwegian Institute of Technology
Spill Frequency	The number of spills of a given spill size range per year. Usually expressed as spills per 1,000 years (and so indicated).
Spill Frequency per Barrel Produced	The number of spills of a given spill size range per barrel produced. Usually expressed as spills per billion barrels produced (and so indicated).
Spill Index	The product of spill frequency for a given spill size range and the mean spill size for that spill size range.
Spill Occurrence	Characterization of an oil spill as an annual frequency and associated spill size or spill size range.
Spill Occurrence Indicator	Any of the oil spill occurrence characteristics; namely, spill frequency, spill frequency per barrel produced, or spill index (defined above).
Spill Sizes	Small (S): 50 - 99 bbl Medium (M): 100 - 999 bbl Large (L): 1,000 - 9,999 bbl Huge (H): >=10,000 bbl Significant (SG): >=1,000 bbl

CHAPTER 1

INTRODUCTION

1.1 General Introduction

The MMS Alaska Outer Continental Shelf (OCS) Region uses oil spill occurrence estimates for National Environmental Policy Act assessments for all parts of their area of jurisdiction, ranging from near shore through shallow water, to deeper water. Although land to 3 nautical miles is not within MMS jurisdiction, it is included in the MMS environmental impact analysis; hence it is also included in the study area here. In 2002 and early 2006, studies were carried out by Bercha International Inc. [11, 12] * to assess and quantify oil spill occurrence indicators for the Beaufort and Chukchi Seas. In this study, methodologies based on fault tree analysis were developed for the assessment of oil spill rates associated with exploration and production facilities and operations in deeper waters in the Chukchi and Beaufort Seas.

The prediction of the reliability (or failure) of systems without history can be approached through a variety of mathematical techniques, with one of the most preferable and accepted being fault trees [7, 10, 14, 23, 26, 45, 51, 65], and their combination with numerical distribution methods such as Monte Carlo simulation [9, 45]. In the previous study [12], fault tree methodology was applied to the prediction of oil spill rates for oil and gas developments such as those now operational or contemplated for the Beaufort and Chukchi Seas in the Alaska OCS, and used to generate predictions of oil spill occurrence indicators.

As there is a paucity of offshore Arctic oil spill occurrences, associated data worldwide and from the Gulf of Mexico (GOM) were used as a starting point to develop a simulation model of oil spill occurrence probabilities. The model for non-Arctic occurrence probabilities was then modified to include Arctic effects and their variabilities. In the preceding Beaufort Sea study [12], variability in the non-Arctic input data was considered; but variability of the future development scenario physical facility parameters, such as miles of sub-sea pipeline, was not considered. In the present study, both the historical data variability and that of the future development scenario characteristics is included in calculation of oil spill occurrence probabilities.

1.2 Study Objectives

The objectives of this study are as follows:

- Assimilate and analyze world-wide and US OCS oil spill statistics and evaluate their applicability to lease tracts which could be offered in the upcoming Chukchi Sea sales.

* Numbers in square brackets refer to citations listed in the "References" section of this report.

- Develop the fault tree method for estimating oil spill occurrences from Chukchi Sea developments associated with spills of different size categories.
- Using the fault tree approach, develop alternative oil spill indicators and assess their variability, including effect of variability of both the historical data the future development scenario parameters.
- Provide statistical support to MMS in evaluation of statistical issues in estimation of oil spill rates.
- One of the specific objectives of this study was to add the variability of the non-Arctic factors.

1.3 Study Area Definition

The geographical study area is the offshore continental shelf in the U.S. Chukchi Sea, as generally illustrated in Figure 1.1. Of interest is the offshore area from landfall to approximately the 60-meter isobath. This area is selected due to the possibility of future oil and gas development within it, based on potential leases. Although a depth greater than 60 meters was originally contemplated as part of the study area, the analysis of development scenarios has indicated that it is highly unlikely that any oil and gas developments will take place in depths greater than 60 meters. More details on the leases and the geology of the study area are described in several MMS publications [35, 36, 37, 38, 39].

Temporally, the study scenarios investigated span into the future from the Year 2009 to 2044.

1.4 General Background

The final reports, dated August 2002 [11] and January 2006 [12], described the methodology and results of the fault tree method for the evaluation of oil spill occurrence estimators for the Beaufort and Chukchi Seas. The focus of the first reports was on the initial development of a fault tree method to model both non-Arctic GOM spill causes as well as Arctic causes and effects that would be encountered in the Beaufort and Chukchi Seas OCS Regions. The variability of the parameters associated with Arctic effects was developed in order to provide an estimate of the variance in the spill occurrence predictions resulting directly from variances in the Arctic effects. In addition, in 2006 [12], variance in the Gulf of Mexico (GOM) historical data was incorporated. However, neither of the two earlier studies [11, 12] considered the variability of the future development scenario parameters. In the present study, this variability is also considered; accordingly, the number of wells and pipeline lengths likely to be installed is included as a distribution rather than as single valued quantities. These variances were numerically incorporated through the use of Monte Carlo simulation for the fault tree model numerical predictions.

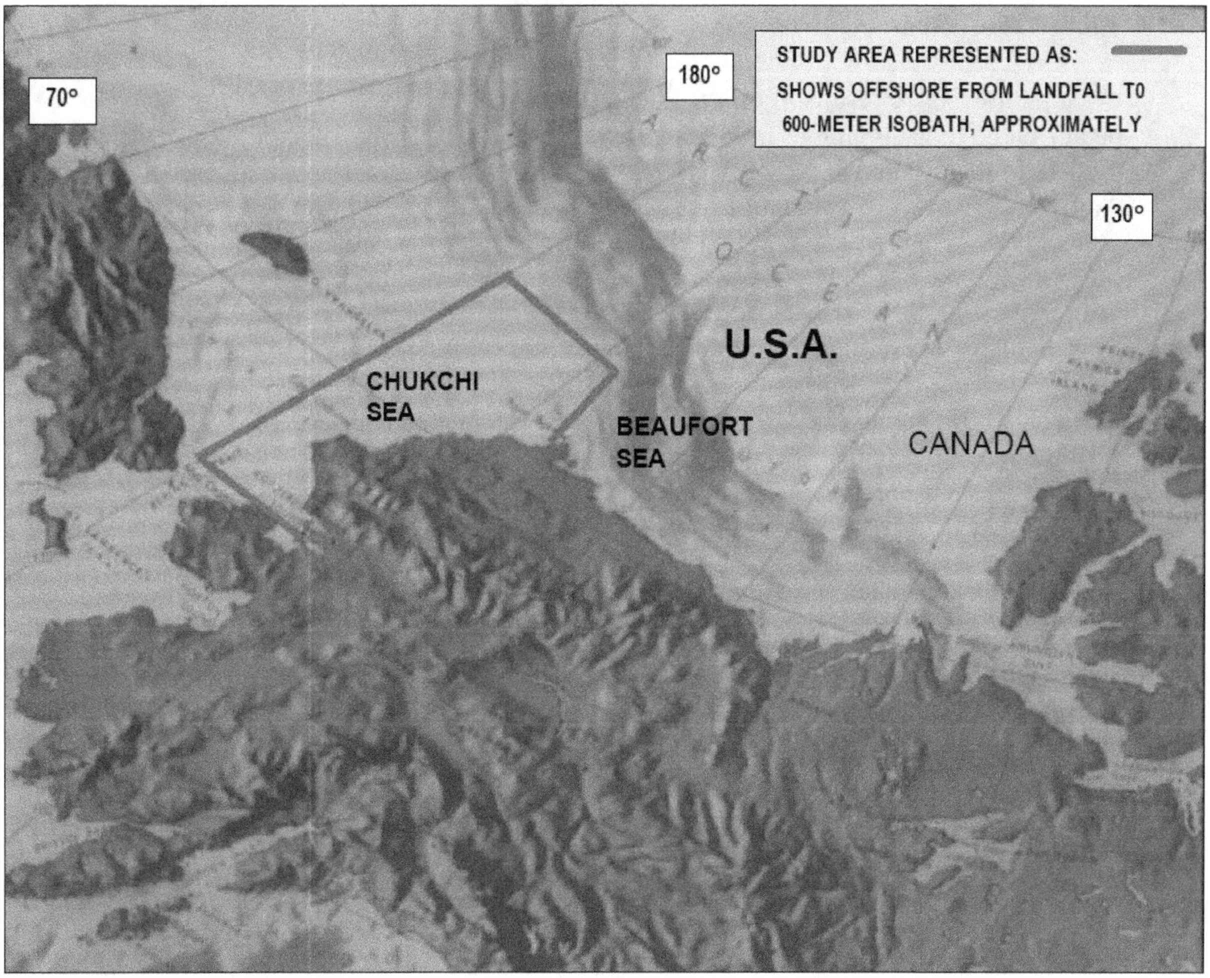

Figure 1.1
Study Area Map

1.5 Technical Approaches

Uncertainties in the results of oil spill occurrence predictions generated in this study can be attributed to uncertainties in input data, scenario characterization, and the occurrence model. In the original 2002 study [11], uncertainties in input data were quantified for the Arctic effects only. Uncertainties in the scenario were included through the choice of scenarios representing the expected and maximum development levels. In the 2006 study [12], uncertainties in the non-Arctic input data were also included. Thus the principal source of uncertainty in the occurrence results was that caused by uncertainties in the Arctic and non-Arctic input parameters themselves.

The non-Arctic input parameters fall under two principal categories as follows:

- Spill frequencies
- Spill volumes

These spill frequencies and volumes as used in the study were derived from the following principal sources:

- Pipeline spills – GOM data
- Platform spills – GOM data
- Well (drilling and production) blowout spills – Worldwide data

The specific sources of the data are described in detail in Chapter 2 of this report.

In the current study, in addition to the above data uncertainties, those of the following main facility parameters were also considered:

- Number of wells drilled
- Number of platforms and sub-sea production wells
- Sub-sea pipeline length
    - For pipelines less than nominal 10" diameter
    - For pipelines greater than or equal to 10" nominal diameter.

The inclusion of all of these types of variability – Arctic effects, non-Arctic data, and facility parameters – is intended to provide a realistic estimate of the spill occurrence indicators and their resultant variability.

1.6 Scope of Work

<u>*Task 1:*</u> *Data Assimilation*

a) Update of GOM pipeline and platform spill data.

b) Identification of alternative data sources including the Foundation of Scientific and Industrial Research at the Norwegian Institute of Technoloty (SINTEF), United Kingdom Health & Safety Executive (HSE), and others.

c) Assimilation and analysis of additional blowout data (SINTEF).

d) Chukchi Sea scenario development from MMS information.

<u>*Task 2:*</u> *Development of Non-Arctic Total Annual Spill Frequency and Volume Probability Distributions*

a) Development of non-Arctic total annual spill frequency and volume distribution for pipelines.

b) Development of non-Arctic total annual spill frequency and volume distribution for platforms.

c) Development of non-Arctic total annual spill frequency and volume distribution for well drilling and production wells.

<u>*Task 3:*</u> *Development of Arctic Spill Frequency Causal Event and Total Probability Distributions*

a) Development of Arctic spill frequency causal event probability distributions associated with pipeline spills.

b) Development of Arctic spill frequency causal event probability distributions associated with platform spills.

c) Development of Arctic spill frequency causal event probability distributions associated with well drilling and production well blowouts.

<u>*Task 4:*</u> *Generation of Oil Spill Occurrence Estimator Probability Distributions*

a) Modification of model to accommodate variability in future development scenario parameters.

b) Model runs for variable Chukchi Sea scenario.

c) Model runs for comparative non-Arctic scenario.

<u>*Task 5:*</u> *Reporting*

a) Preliminary results following completion of Tasks 1, 2, 3, and 4.

b) Draft Final Report and Final Report.

1.7 Work Organization

The present study consisted of statistical and engineering investigations, followed by numerical simulation. Although the assimilation of historical and future scenario data is of key significance to the work, the salient contribution consisted primarily of the analytical work involving fault trees and oil spill occurrence indicator generation. Although the individual calculations are relatively simple, the subdivision of the calculations into realistic representative categories of facilities, spill sizes, and water depth for different variable development scenarios resulted in a relatively complex mix of computations, generally illustrated in the flow chart in Figure 1.2.

The flow chart in Figure 1.2, of course, does not show all the different combinations and permutations; rather, it indicates the typical calculations for one case, and suggests the balance by dotted lines. Moving from left to right; initially historical data were obtained for each of three principal facility categories, pipelines, platforms, and wells. Pipelines were further subdivided among < 10 inch and >=10 inch diameter lines. Wells were categorized in two ways: according to producing (production) wells and the drilling (D) of exploration and development wells. For each of the above facility subcategories, spill causes were analyzed for small, medium, large, huge, and significant spills, defined as follows:

- Small (S) - 50 to 99 bbl
- Medium (M) - 100 to 999 bbl
- Large (L) - 1,000 to 9,999 bbl
- Huge (H) - >= 10,000 bbl
- Significant (SG) - >= 1,000 bbl

Significant spills, which are spills of 1,000 bbl or more (Large and Huge) are also identified. Fractional spill sizes were rounded up or down to the nearest whole number, with rounding up for any decimal ending in 5. For example, a spill of 99.5 bbl is taken as 100 bbl; 99.42 is taken as 99 bbl.

In the interests of conciseness and clarity, the above main categories of spill sizes will generally be designated by either their name (small, medium, large, huge, significant) or, when space is limited, by their acronym (S, M, L, H, SG), in the balance of this report.

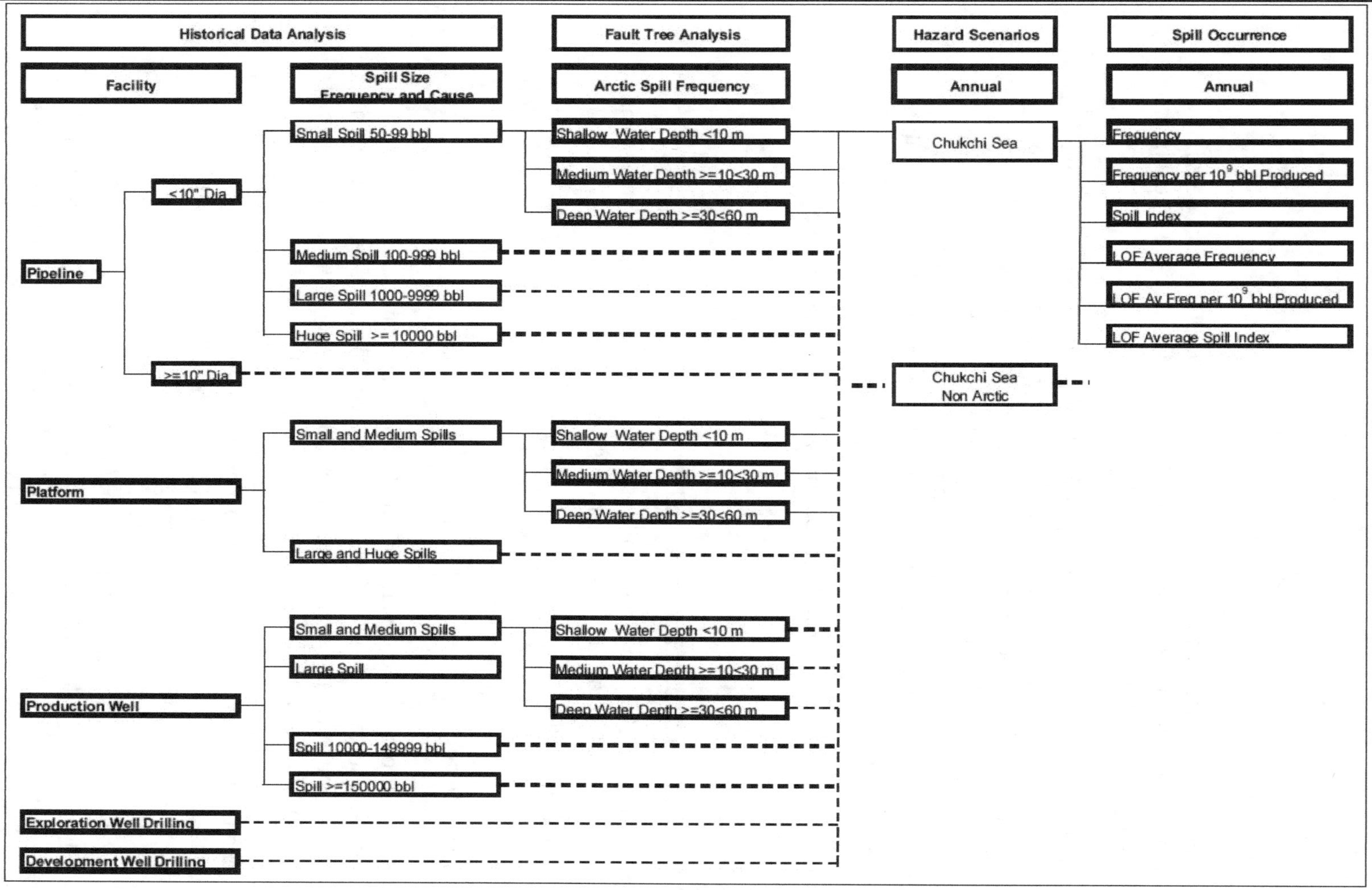
Historical Data Analysis
Fault Tree Analysis
Hazard Scenarios
Spill Occurrence
Facility
Spill Size Frequency and Cause
Arctic Spill Frequency
Annual
Annual
Pipeline
<10" Dia
>=10" Dia
Small Spill 50-99 bbl
Medium Spill 100-999 bbl
Large Spill 1000-9999 bbl
Huge Spill >= 10000 bbl
Shallow Water Depth <10 m
Medium Water Depth >=10<30 m
Deep Water Depth >=30<60 m
Chukchi Sea
Chukchi Sea Non Arctic
Frequency
Frequency per 10^9 bbl Produced
Spill Index
LOF Average Frequency
LOF Av Freq per 10^9 bbl Produced
LOF Average Spill Index
Platform
Small and Medium Spills
Large and Huge Spills
Shallow Water Depth <10 m
Medium Water Depth >=10<30 m
Deep Water Depth >=30<60 m
Production Well
Small and Medium Spills
Large Spill
Spill 10000-149999 bbl
Spill >=150000 bbl
Shallow Water Depth <10 m
Medium Water Depth >=10<30 m
Deep Water Depth >=30<60 m
Exploration Well Drilling
Development Well Drilling

Figure 1.2
Calculation Flow Chart

Next, in the frequency analysis utilizing fault trees, each of three representative water depth ranges was assessed as follows:

- Shallow - < 10 meters
- Medium - 10 to 29 meters
- Deep - 30 to 60 meters

Although originally it was anticipated that 'very deep' water would be considered, it was found that none of the development scenarios anticipated by MMS for the Chukchi Sea extended beyond the 60-meter isobath.

One principal future development scenario was defined for the Chukchi Sea, as well as a compatible non-Arctic (hypothetical) scenario. Each scenario was described for each year in its development history, from the year 2009 to the year 2044. The hypothetical non-Arctic scenario was developed for comparative purposes on the assumption that it was located with the same facility distribution in a non-Arctic area. This permitted the comparison of the spill indicator results with and without the application of the fault tree analysis to account for Arctic effects.

Finally, for each of the scenarios considered, four oil spill occurrence indicators were generated, as follows:

- Oil spill frequency
- Oil spill frequency per barrel produced
- Spill index, which is the product of the oil spill frequency and the mean spill size (for the particular category under consideration)
- Life of Field Indices

1.8 Outline of Report

Following this brief introductory chapter, Volume I of the final report addresses each of the principal tasks and subtasks in its logical sequence. Accordingly, Chapter 2 describes the historical data assimilation and analysis, Chapter 3 defines the future development scenario used, Chapter 4 discusses the fault tree analysis to obtain Arctic oil spill frequencies, while Chapter 5 summarizes the results of the oil spill occurrence indicator computations and their distributions. Chapter 6 summarizes conclusions and recommendations including a section on the benefits and shortcomings of the present study. Extensive references and bibliography are given in the References.

The appendices given in Volume II form an integral part of the work for the reader who wishes to learn about background and calculation details. Accordingly, Appendix 1 summarizes the historical data assimilated and analyzed. Appendix 2 gives details of the fault tree analysis. Appendix 3 gives details on the future development scenario utilized as a basis for the study. Appendix 4 gives a printout of all the calculation steps, including results, utilized in the development of the Arctic oil spill occurrence indicators using the Monte Carlo approach. Appendix 5 gives general conclusions and results. The appendices are provided in pdf format on a CD-ROM.

CHAPTER 2

HISTORICAL DATA

2.1 Approaches to Historical Data

Historical data on offshore oil spills were utilized as a numerical starting point for predicting Arctic offshore oil spill characteristics. Because a statistical history on Arctic offshore oil spills does not exist, oil spill histories for temperate offshore locations were utilized. Although Arctic offshore exploration and production was started in the early 1970s, operations have been sporadic, with very few spills, so that a statistical history cannot be generated.

The following data sets or databases were utilized:

(a) GOM OCS Pipeline Spills (1972-1999)
(b) GOM OCS Platform Spills (1972-1999)
(c) Oil Blowouts, Worldwide (1955-1995)

The above categories of data are discussed and summarized in Appendix 1. The contents of the balance of this chapter are restricted to the presentation and discussion of only those data sets utilized in the present study.

2.2 Pipeline Oil Spill Data

The MMS database called *PPL_REPAIRS* was used as a basis for the assessment of subsea pipeline oil spills [2]. This database contains records of all reported spills in the GOM. The database was used to obtain spill records for spills of 50 bbl or more between January 1st, 1972 and December 31st, 1999. The 32 spills reported in this date range were further subdivided into volume, pipeline diameter, pipeline segment length, and pipeline segment depth ranges as summarized in Table 2.1.

Next, 32 GOM OCS pipeline spill records were reviewed and analyzed for causal and spill size distributions. Table 2.2 shows the summary of the causal record information, while Table 2.3 summarizes the spill cause distributions for two spill size ranges (small and medium, large and huge). Finally, Table 2.4 gives the principal parameters of the spill population for pipelines. The "Historical" value is the historical average value from Table 2.1; the low value is the most common annual low value (0 spills), and the high value is the approximate upper 90% confidence interval value.

Table 2.1
GOM OCS Pipeline Spills Statistics Summary (1972-1999)
(App. Table 1.3)

GOM OCS Pipeline Spills, Categorized 1972-99			Spill Statistics	Exposure	Frequency
			Number of Spills	km-years	Spills per 10^5 km-years
By Pipe Diameter*		< 10"	16	105,336	15.1894
		>= 10"	16	81,847	19.5488
By Spill Size		Small 50-99 bbl	6	187,183	3.2054
		Medium 100 - 999 bbl	13	187,183	6.9451
		Large 1000 - 9999 bbl	10	187,183	5.3424
		Huge >=10000 bbl	3	187,183	1.6027
By Diameter, By Spill Size	< 10"	Small 50-99 bbl	4	105,336	3.7974
		Medium 100 - 999 bbl	7	105,336	6.6454
		Large 1000 - 9999 bbl	4	105,336	3.7974
		Huge >=10000 bbl	1	105,336	0.9493
	>= 10"	Small <100 bbl	2	81,847	2.4436
		Medium 100 - 999 bbl	6	81,847	7.3308
		Large 1000 - 9999 bbl	6	81,847	7.3308
		Huge >=10000 bbl	2	81,847	2.4436

*14 of the 32 records have both MIN_WATER_DEPTH and MAX_WATER_DEPTH set to "0".

Table 2.2
Analysis of GOM OCS Pipeline Spill Data for Causal Distribution and Spill Size
(App.Table 1.1)

CAUSE CLASSIFICATION	# OF SPILLS	SPILL SIZE BBL										NUMBER OF SPILLS					
		1	2	3	4	5	6	7	8	9	10	S	M	L	H	SM	LH
CORROSION	**4**											**1**	**2**	**1**		**3**	**1**
External	1	80										1				**1**	
nternal	3	100	5000	414									2	1		**2**	**1**
THIRD PARTY IMPACT	**16**											**2**	**5**	**6**	**3**	**7**	**9**
Anchor Impact	10	19833	65	50	300	900	323	15576	2000	800	1211	2	4	2	2	**6**	**4**
Jackup Rig or Spud Barge	1	3200												1			**1**
Trawl/Fishing Net	5	4000	100	14423	4569	4533							1	3	1	**1**	**4**
OPERATION IMPACT	**4**											**3**		**1**		**3**	**1**
Rig Anchoring	1	50										1				**1**	
Work Boat Anchoring	3	50	5100	50								2		1		**2**	**1**
MECHANICAL	**2**												**2**			**2**	
Connection Failure	1	135											1			**1**	
Material Failure	1	210											1			**1**	
NATURAL HAZARD	**4**											**1**	**1**	**2**		**2**	**2**
Mud Slide	3	250	80	8212								1	1	1		**2**	**1**
Storm/ Hurricane	1	3500												1			**1**
ARCTIC																	
ce Gouging																	
Strudel Scour																	
Upheaval Buckling																	
Thaw Settlement																	
Other																	
UNKNOWN	**2**	119	190										**2**			**2**	
TOTALS	**32**											**7**	**12**	**10**	**3**	**19**	**13**

Table 2.3
Distribution and Frequency of Historical Spills – Pipeline
(App. Table 1.2)

CAUSE CLASSIFICATION	Small and Medium Spills 50-999 bbl				Large and Huge Spills >=1000 bbl			
	HISTORICAL DISTRI-BUTION %	NUMBER OF SPILLS	EXPOSURE [km-years]	FREQUENCY spill per 10^5km-year	HISTORICAL DISTRI-BUTION %	NUMBER OF SPILLS	EXPOSURE [km-years]	FREQUENCY spill per 10^5 km-year
CORROSION	**15.79**	**3**		**1.6027**	**7.69**	**1**		**0.5342**
External	5.26	1		0.5342				
Internal	10.53	2		1.0685	7.69	1		0.5342
THIRD PARTY IMPACT	**36.84**	**7**		**3.7397**	**69.23**	**9**		**4.8081**
Anchor Impact	31.58	6		3.2054	30.77	4		2.1369
Jackup Rig or Spud Barge					7.69	1		0.5342
Trawl/Fishing Net	5.26	1		0.5342	30.77	4		2.1369
OPERATION IMPACT	**15.79**	**3**		**1.6027**	**7.69**	**1**		**0.5342**
Rig Anchoring	5.26	1		0.5342				
Work Boat Anchoring	10.53	2		1.0685	7.69	1		0.5342
MECHANICAL	**10.53**	**2**		**1.0685**				
Connection Failure	5.26	1	187183	0.5342			187183	
Material Failure	5.26	1		0.5342				
NATURAL HAZARD	**10.53**	**2**		**1.0685**	**15.38**	**2**		**1.0685**
Mud Slide	10.53	2		1.0685	7.69	1		0.5342
Storm/ Hurricane					7.69	1		0.5342
ARCTIC								
Ice Gouging								
Strudel Scour								
Upheaval Buckling								
Thaw Settlement								
Other								
UNKNOWN	**10.53**	**2**		**1.0685**				
TOTALS	**100.00**	**19**		**10.1505**	**100.00**	**13**		**6.9451**

Table 2.4
Pipeline Historical Spill Frequency Variability

GOM OCS Pipeline Spills, Categorized 1972-99		Frequency spill per 10^5 km-years			
		Historical	Low	Mode	High
By Diameter, By Spill Size					
< 10"	Small	3.7974	0	1.6329	9.7592
	Medium	6.6454	0	2.8575	17.0786
	Large	3.7974	0	1.6329	9.7592
	Huge	0.9493	0	0.4082	2.4398
= 10"	Small	2.4436	0	1.0507	6.2800
	Medium	6.1090	0	2.6269	15.7001
	Large	7.3308	0	3.1522	18.8401
	Huge	2.4436	0	1.0507	6.2800

For example, if there were 30 data points, the upper 90% (or high value) was the third highest, while the lower 90% (or low value) was selected as the third lowest, which was invariably zero, as numerous years had no spills. Next, the third highest value was divided by the historical value to get the high factor. Finally, the high factor was used to obtain the high value by multiplying the applicable historical frequency by this high factor. The mode was then calculated from the triangular distribution relationship [13], as follows:

$$\textit{Mode} = 3 \times \textit{Historical} - \textit{High} - \textit{Low} \qquad \textbf{(2.1)}$$

2.3 Platform Spill Data

Platform spills in the MMS database are given for the period from 1972 to 1999 [2]. The platform spill data are given for an exposure of producing well-years. As for pipelines, the spill records themselves were accessed in order to obtain the correlation between spill cause and spill size. Table 2.5 shows the results of the causal and spill size distribution analysis, while Table 2.6 gives the causal distribution as well as the spill frequency per 10,000 well-years. Finally, Table 2.7 gives the principal variability parameters of the spill population for platforms. The high values were chosen as the annual spill rates closest to the upper and lower 90% confidence interval, and calculated as described in Section 2.2; the low value is zero.

In order to assess spill occurrence from platform facilities, using the above per well-year frequency, it is necessary to estimate the number of wells per platform. For the Chukchi Sea scenario, there is only one platform to which all production wells were attributed as on-platform or subsea wells tied to the platform with umbilicals.

2.4 Oil Well Blowout Data

The development scenarios considered under this study include both the drilling of exploratory and development wells, and the production wells producing oil. To identify a basis for the non-Arctic historical oil well blowout statistics, a number of sources were reviewed including the Northstar and Liberty oil development project reports [52], a study by ScanPower giving the cumulative distribution function for oil blowout releases [59], as well as the book by Per Holand entitled "Offshore Blowouts", which gives risk analysis data from the SINTEF worldwide offshore blowout database [25]. The most comprehensive historical information was found in the latter reference [25], which not only gives the results of database analyses for the North Sea and the Gulf of Mexico, but also provides confidence intervals calculated from these databases. Table 2.8 gives a summary of the historical data analysis by Per Holland [25] for production wells and the drilling of exploratory and development wells. The combination of these statistics together with the cumulative distribution function for oil blowout release volumes given in [59], generated in support of the Northstar project, permits the blowout spill volume frequency distribution as summarized in Table 2.9. Finally, combining the population parameters of oil well blowouts from Table 2.8 with the size distribution factors – which can be derived from Table 2.9 – one arrives at the historical oil spill blowout distribution characteristics by spill size and well type, summarized in Table 2.10.

Table 2.5
Analysis of GOM OCS Platform Spill Data for Causal Distribution and Spill Size (1972-1999)
(App.Table 1.5)

CAUSE CLASSIFICATION	# OF SPILLS	SPILL SIZE BBL													NUMBER OF SPILLS					
		1	2	3	4	5	6	7	8	9	10	11	12	13	S	M	L	H	SM	LH
PROCESS FACILITY RLS.	13	130	50	120	104	60	1456	125	50	50	55	400	280	75	6	6	1		12	1
STORAGE TANK RLS.	3	9935	7000	435												1	2		1	2
STRUCTURAL FAILURE	1	58													1				1	
HURRICANE/STORM	2	75	66												2				2	
COLLISION	2	600	108													2			2	
TOTALS	***21***														***9***	***9***	***3***		***18***	***3***

Table 2.6
Causal and Spill Size Distribution of GOM OCS Platform Spills (1972-1999)
(App. Table 1.6)

CAUSE CLASSIFICATION	Small and Medium Spills				Large and Huge Spills			
	HIST. DISTRI-BUTION (%)	# OF SPILLS	EXPOSURE (well-yr)	FREQUENCY (spill per 10^4 well-yr)	HIST. DISTRI-BUTION (%)	# OF SPILLS	EXPOSURE (well-yr)	FREQUENCY (spill per 10^4 well-yr)
PROCESS FACILITY RLS.	66.67	12	119714	1.0024	33.33	1	119714	0.0835
STORAGE TANK RLS.	5.56	1		0.0835	66.67	2		0.1671
STRUCTURAL FAILURE	5.56	1		0.0835				
HURRICANE/STORM	11.11	2		0.1671				
COLLISION	11.11	2		0.1671				
TOTALS	***100.00***	***18***		***1.5036***	***100.00***	***3***		***0.2506***

Table 2.7
Platform Historical Spill Frequency Variability

Spill Size	Frequency Unit	Historical	Low	Mode	High
Small and Medium Spills 50-999 bbl	**spill per 10^4 well-year**	1.5036	0.0000	0.1804	4.3303
Large and Huge Spills >=1000 bbl	**spill per 10^4 well-year**	0.2506	0.0000	0.0301	0.7217

Table 2.8
Summary of North Sea and Gulf of Mexico Blowout Rates
(Holand, 1997)

Well Type	Unit	Low 90% CI	Average	High 90% CI
Production Well	Spills per 10^4 well-year	0.86	1.91	2.95
Exploration Well Drilling	Spills per 10^4 wells	11.00	25.05	51.00
Development Well Drilling		4.00	9.15	16.10

Table 2.9
Well Blowout Historical Spill Size Distribution
(ScanPower, 2001) *(App. Table 1.8)*

EVENT	FREQUENCY UNIT	HISTORICAL FREQUENCY					
		Small and Medium Spills 50-999 bbl	Large Spills 1000-9999 bbl	Small, Medium, and Large Spills 50-9999 bbl	Spills 10000-149999 bbl	Spills >=150000 bbl	All spills
PRODUCTION WELL	spills per 10^4 well-year	0.15	1.03	1.18	0.44	0.29	1.91
EXPLORATION WELL DRILLING	spills per 10^4 wells	1.97	13.75	15.72	5.91	3.42	25.05
DEVELOPMENT WELL DRILLING	spills per 10^4 wells	0.65	4.57	5.22	1.96	1.96	9.15

Table 2.10
Well Blowout Historical Spill Probability and Size Variability
(App. Table 1.9)

EVENT	FREQUENCY UNIT	Low Factor	High Factor	Frequencies			
				Historical	Low	Mode	High
				Small and Medium Spills 50-999 bbl			
PRODUCTION WELL	spill per 10^4 well-year	0.448	1.545	0.147	0.066	0.148	0.227
EXPLORATION WELL DRILLING	spill per 10^4 wells	0.439	2.036	1.966	0.863	1.032	4.002
DEVELOPMENT WELL DRILLING	spill per 10^4 wells	0.437	1.760	0.654	0.286	0.526	1.151
				Large Spills 1000-9999 bbl			
PRODUCTION WELL	spill per 10^4 well-year	0.448	1.545	1.028	0.460	1.037	1.588
EXPLORATION WELL DRILLING	spill per 10^4 wells	0.439	2.036	13.754	6.039	7.220	28.001
DEVELOPMENT WELL DRILLING	spill per 10^4 wells	0.437	1.760	4.570	1.998	3.671	8.041
				Small, Medium and Large Spills 50-9999 bbl			
PRODUCTION WELL	spill per 10^4 well-year	0.448	1.545	1.175	0.526	1.185	1.815
EXPLORATION WELL DRILLING	spill per 10^4 wells	0.439	2.036	15.719	6.903	8.252	32.003
DEVELOPMENT WELL DRILLING	spill per 10^4 wells	0.437	1.760	5.224	2.284	4.197	9.192
				Spill 10000-149999 bbl			
PRODUCTION WELL	spill per 10^4 well-year	0.448	1.545	0.441	0.197	0.444	0.681
EXPLORATION WELL DRILLING	spill per 10^4 wells	0.439	2.036	5.909	2.595	3.102	12.031
DEVELOPMENT WELL DRILLING	spill per 10^4 wells	0.437	1.760	1.963	0.858	1.577	3.454
				Spill >=150000 bbl			
PRODUCTION WELL	spill per 10^4 well-year	0.448	1.545	0.294	0.132	0.296	0.454
EXPLORATION WELL DRILLING	spill per 10^4 wells	0.439	2.036	3.421	1.502	1.796	6.965
DEVELOPMENT WELL DRILLING	spill per 10^4 wells	0.437	1.760	1.963	0.858	1.577	3.454

2.5 Arctic Effects Historical Data

2.5.1 General Approaches to the Quantification of Arctic Effects

There are essentially two main categories of Arctic effects; namely, those that are unique to the Arctic, such as marine ice effects, and those that are the same types of effects as those in temperate areas, but occurring with a different frequency, such as anchor impacts on subsea pipelines. The first will be termed "unique" effects; the second, "modified" effects. Modified Arctic effects are dealt with in conjunction with the fault tree analysis described in Chapter 4. Only those Arctic effects or hazards unique to the Arctic, and potentially having a historical occurrence database, such as ice gouging, are discussed in the balance of this section.

2.5.2 Ice Gouging

Ice gouging occurs when a moving ice feature contacts the sea bottom and penetrates into it, generally as it moves against a positive sea bottom slope. The ice feature can be a multiyear ridge, a hummock, or ice rafting formation. Various studies have been conducted on the frequency and depth distribution of ice gouges [8, 27, 29, 30, 46, 67, 68], and a number of assessments of the likelihood of resultant subsea pipeline failure [8, 29] have also been carried out. Pipeline failure frequencies at different water depth regimes as a result of ice gouging in this study have been estimated on the basis of the historical ice gouge characteristics [29] together with an analytical assessment [8, 68] of their likelihood to damage a pipeline.

According to Weeks [67, 68], a relationship between the expected probability of pipeline failure from ice gouging and ice gouging local characteristics may be expressed as follows:

$$N = e^{-kx} H_S \; ? \; F \; ? \; T \; ? \; L_P \; ? \; \sin ? \qquad \textbf{(2.2)}$$

Where:

N	=	Number of pipeline failures at burial depth of cover x (meters)
k	=	Inverse of mean scour depth (m^{-1})
x	=	Depth of cover (m)
H_S	=	Probability of pipeline failure given ice gouge impact or hit
F	=	Scour flux per km-yr
T	=	Exposure time (years)
L_P	=	Length of pipeline (km)
?	=	Gouge orientation (degrees) from pipeline centerline

For the Northstar project, according to [30], the mean scour depth is 0.2 m giving a ***k*** factor of 5.0. In addition, a good estimate of scour flux for shallow water is 2 gouges/km-yr. Using an average pipeline depth of cover of 2.5 m, an average directional angle of 45°, a conditional failure probability (H_S) of 0.83, gives a frequency of 5.26 x 10^{-6}/km-yr. For the purposes of the analysis, this frequency must be distributed among different spill size consequences. Due to the difficulty of detecting spills under ice, one can expect that the majority of spills would be in the large and huge categories. However, huge spills would be limited by segment length. Thus, a conditional probability (given a spill) of 50% has been assigned to large spills, and one of 14% to huge spills. Least likely are small spills, and accordingly they have been given a probability of 13%. The remaining probability of 23% has been assigned to medium sized spills. The resultant distribution of expected frequencies of spill sizes associated with ice gouging is given in Table 2.11.

Also, high and low values have been assigned in order to permit an analysis of the likely distribution of the effects. Essentially, these variations in effect probability were obtained through a parametric sensitivity analysis using Equation 2.1 for a range of likely values of depth of cover from 2.0 m to 3.0 m (with an expected value of2.5 m). These resultant low and high values are also summarized in Table 2.11. For medium water depth (10 to 29 m), an analogous process was carried out with a reduced gouge flux of 1.5 gouges/km-yr. For deep water (>= 30 m) no gouging is expected.

2.5.3 Strudel Scour

When water collects on top of the landfast ice, generally from rivers running into the Arctic seas, and drains through a hole in the ice, its hydrodynamic effect on the ocean floor below forms a depression which is called a strudel scour. Numerous studies have been conducted on strudel scour [29, 30], so that a prediction on the number of strudel scours per unit area can be made on the basis of historical data. Strudel scours are restricted to shallow water. With an average strudel scour frequency of 4 scours/mi^2 (1.5 scours/km^2) [30], the methodology in [30] can be utilized to predict a possible failure rate of subsea pipelines in shallow waters due to strudel scour of approximately 8.9 x 10^{-8}/km-yr. Using reasoning similar to that for the distribution of spill sizes for ice gouging, and assigning limits based on parametric sensitivity studies, the distribution of strudel scour frequencies for shallow water as shown in Table 2.11 can be derived. Strudel scours are not expected in water depths greater than 10 m.

Table 2.11
Summary of Pipeline Unique Arctic Effect Inputs
(App. Table 2.2)

Cause Classification	Spill Size	Water Depth								
		Shallow			Medium			Deep		
		Frequency Increment per 10^5 km-year								
		Min	Mode	Max	Min	Mode	Max	Min	Mode	Max
Ice Gouging	S	0.0060	0.0680	0.8290	0.0048	0.0544	0.6632			
	M	0.0090	0.1210	1.4670	0.0072	0.0968	1.1736			
	L	0.0210	0.2610	3.1900	0.0168	0.2088	2.5520			
	H	0.0060	0.0730	0.8930	0.0048	0.0584	0.7144			
Strudel Scour	S	0.0004	0.0012	0.0044						
	M	0.0006	0.0020	0.0078						
	L	0.0014	0.0045	0.0170						
	H	0.0004	0.0012	0.0048						
Upheaval Buckling	S	0.00007	0.00023	0.00088	0.00007	0.00023	0.00088	0.00007	0.00023	0.00088
	M	0.00013	0.00041	0.00156	0.00013	0.00041	0.00156	0.00013	0.00041	0.00156
	L	0.00028	0.00089	0.00340	0.00028	0.00089	0.00340	0.00028	0.00089	0.00340
	H	0.00008	0.00025	0.00095	0.00008	0.00025	0.00095	0.00008	0.00025	0.00095
Thaw Settlement	S	0.00000	0.00000	0.00000	0.00000	0.00000	0.00000	0.00000	0.00000	0.00000
	M	0.00000	0.00000	0.00000	0.00000	0.00000	0.00000	0.00000	0.00000	0.00000
	L	0.00000	0.00000	0.00000	0.00000	0.00000	0.00000	0.00000	0.00000	0.00000
	H	0.00000	0.00000	0.00000	0.00000	0.00000	0.00000	0.00000	0.00000	0.00000
Other	S	0.00162	0.01738	0.20869	0.00123	0.01369	0.16613	0.00003	0.00009	0.00033
	M	0.00246	0.03092	0.36929	0.00185	0.02435	0.29399	0.00005	0.00015	0.00059
	L	0.00571	0.06670	0.80303	0.00431	0.05253	0.63928	0.00011	0.00033	0.00128
	H	0.00163	0.01865	0.22480	0.00123	0.01469	0.17896	0.00003	0.00009	0.00036

2.5.4 Upheaval Buckling

Upheaval buckling occurs in a pipeline as a result of its thermal expansion which causes it to buckle upwards to accommodate the extra length generated from thermal effects. Unfortunately, there appears to be no defensible analytical method for calculating the probability of upheaval buckling of Arctic subsea pipelines in general. Accordingly, upheaval buckling has been taken simply as a percentage of the strudel scour effects. Assuming that a upheaval buckling occurs 20% as often as strudel scour, the distribution shown in Table 2.9 can be derived. Upheaval buckling is expected to be independent of water depth; accordingly, the same values have been used for each water depth range.

2.5.5 Thaw Settlement

Thaw settlement occurs when a permafrost lens or formation over which the pipeline was installed melts as a result of the heat generated by the pipeline and ceases to support the pipeline so that the pipeline overburden loads the pipeline and causes it to deflect downwards. As there are no permafrost strata in the Chukchi study area, no thaw settlement is expected.

2.5.6 Platform Arctic Unique Effects

Potential causes of platform spills (other than blowouts, which are included under wells) that are uniquely associated with the Arctic are ice forces and low temperature effects. Although the possibility that ice forces will cause spills varies greatly from facility to facility, some broad assumptions have been made in regards to the likelihood of spills being caused by ice force effects. Specifically, it was assumed that the platforms are designed for a 10,000 year return period with a reliability level of 96%, in accordance with the Draft ISO WG8 Arctic Structures Reliability Section 7.2.2.3 [28]. That is, 4% of the time, the 10,000 year return period ice force can cause a spill. Further, it was assumed that 85% of spills so caused are small and medium, with large and huge spills associated with the other 15%. In regards to facility low temperature, a percentage of historical facility releases was taken. Specifically, it was assumed that the facility low temperature effects will cause medium spills at a rate of 6% of that of total historical small and medium spills, and large and huge spills at a rate of 3% of that associated with large and huge historical spills. Finally, other Arctic unique causes were assumed to constitute another 10% of the sum of the above spill rates in each of the spill categories. Table 2.12 summarizes the resultant Arctic unique effect frequencies derived for platforms on a per-well year basis.

Table 2.12
Summary of Platform Unique Arctic Effect Inputs
(App. Table 2.8)

CAUSE	SPILL SIZE	FREQUENCY INCREMENT PER 10^4 well-year (Mode)			REASON
		Shallow	Medium	Deep	
Ice Force	Small, Medium	0.0340	0.0510	0.0765	Assumed 10,000 year return period ice force causes spill 4% occurrences (96% reliability). 85% of the spills are Small/Medium.
	Large, Huge	0.0060	0.0090	0.0135	
Facility Low Temperature	Small, Medium	0.1000	0.1000	0.1000	Assumed fraction of Historical Process Facilities release frequency with 6% for Small/Medium and 3% for Large/Huge spill sizes.
	Large, Huge	0.0080	0.0080	0.0080	
Other	Small, Medium	0.0134	0.0151	0.0177	10% of sum of above.
	Large, Huge	0.0014	0.0017	0.0022	

2.6 Historical Spill Size Distribution

Table 2.13 gives the historical spill size distributions obtained from the available historical data. Here, the mode was taken as the historical average spill size in each spill size category, while the high and low values were taken to be the upper and lower bounds of each spill size category. The Huge spill high values were chosen on the basis of the upper 90% confidence interval spill volumes in the databases.

Table 2.13
Summary of Historical Spill Size Distribution Parameters

PIPELINE SPILL VOLUMES	**Spill Size**	**Small Spills (50-99 bbl)**			**Medium Spills (100-999 bbl)**			**Large Spills (1,000-9,999 bbl)**			**Huge Spills (= 10,000 bbl)**		
	Spill Expectation	**Low**	**Mode**	**High**	**Low**	**Mode**	**High**	**Low**	**Mode**	**High**	**Low**	**Mode**	**High**
	Pipeline (Diameter <10") Spill	50	58	99	100	226	999	1000	4436	9999	10000	14423	20000
	Pipeline (Diameter >10") Spill	50	58	99	100	387	999	1000	3932	9999	10000	17705	20000
PLATFORM SPILL VOLUMES	**Spill Size**	**Small and Medium Spills (50-999 bbl)**			**Large and Huge Spills (= 1,000 bbl)**								
	Spill Expectation	**Low**	**Mode**	**High**	**Low**	**Mode**	**High**						
	Platform Spill	50	158	999	1000	6130	10000						
WELL SPILL VOLUMES	**Spill Size**	**Small and Medium Spills (50-999 bbl)**			**Large Spills (1,000-9,999 bbl)**			**Spills (10,000-149,999 bbl)**			**Spills (= 150,000 bbl)**		
	Spill Expectation	**Low**	**Mode**	**High**	**Low**	**Mode**	**High**	**Low**	**Mode**	**High**	**Low**	**Mode**	**High**
	Well Spill	50	500	999	1000	4500	9999	10000	20000	149999	150000	200000	250000

CHAPTER 3

FUTURE DEVELOPMENT SCENARIOS

3.1 Approaches to Future Development Scenarios

For the purposes of the fault tree analysis utilized in this study, future Chukchi Sea offshore oil and gas development scenarios need to include the following characteristics for each year of the development scenario:

- Water depth range for pipelines
- Physical quantities of individual facilities (e.g., production wells, pipelines) on an annual basis in correspondence with the baseline data exposure factors (e.g., per well year or per km-yr)
- Associated oil production volumes
- Other characteristics such as pipeline diameter or type of well drilled

Table 3.1 shows the classification of development Scenarios by water depth range and operation type. The salient aspect of this classification is subdivision into water depth ranges among which Arctic hazard characteristics (such as ice gouging rates) may change. The following water depth categories are used:

- Shallow - < 10 meters
- Medium - 10 to 29 meters
- Deep - 30 to 60 meters
- Very Deep - > 60 meters

In Table 3.1, an indication is given of the types of facilities that might be utilized in each of the principal types of oil and gas activities, exploration, production, or transportation. As will be seen in this chapter, current forecasts for development scenarios over the next 40 years exclude very deep locations, in excess of 60 m. Accordingly, any suggestions for facilities under the very deep scenario would be speculative and will not be used in the current study.

In general, the scenarios described in this chapter were developed to an appropriate level and type of detail to match the type of unit spill data and statistics available as a basis for the oil spill occurrence indicator quantification.

The principal regions of interest within the study area are the Chukchi Sea lease areas.

Table 3.1
Classification of Development Scenarios

PRINCIPAL ACTIVITY	WATER DEPTH (m)			
	SHALLOW (< 10)	MEDIUM (10 to 29)	DEEP (30 to 60)	VERY DEEP (> 60)
EXPLORATION	▪ Artificial island ▪ Drill barge ▪ Ice island	▪ Artificial island ▪ Drill ship (summer) ▪ Caisson	▪ Drill ship (summer) ▪ Semisubmersible (summer)	▪ Drill ship (summer) ▪ Semisubmersible (summer)
PRODUCTION	▪ Artificial island ▪ Caisson island	▪ Caisson island ▪ Gravity Base Structure (GBS)	▪ Caisson island ▪ Gravity Base Structure (GBS)	▪ New design structure ▪ Submarine habitat
TRANSPORT	▪ Subsea pipeline	▪ Subsea pipeline	▪ Subsea pipeline ▪ Storage & tankers	▪ Subsea pipeline ▪ Submarine storage ▪ Icebreaking tankers ▪ Submarine tankers

3.2 Chukchi Sea Development Scenarios

As a basis for the current analysis, the geographic and water depth distribution of the facilities and its variation over the life of the development is required in order to effectively incorporate the effects of Arctic operations on the oil spill occurrences. Table 3.2 summarizes the key quantity parameters of a possible Chukchi scenario. The facility quantities are hypothetical, and not based on any operator's plan. No facilities are predicted in the very deep region.

Table 3.3 summarizes the complete development scenario including its temporal development from 2009 to Year 2044, at which time it is forecast to cease production. For items such as exploration and field delineation well drilling, the actual number of wells drilled in a given year were needed, since the statistics of well spill (blowouts) are on a per well drilled exposure unit. For items that continue from year to year, such as production wells or subsea pipelines, both the annual incremental and the cumulative total are needed. Specifically, the following facility quantities were estimated and distributed as shown in Table 3.3:

- Exploration wells drilled – annual
- Delineation wells drilled – annual
- Production platforms – only one platform was assumed
- Production/service wells – annual increment and cumulative number
- Pipeline lengths for < 10", and >=10", and total – annual increment and cumulative number of pipeline length in service
- Oil production volumes – annual

As noted above, these quantities match the type of unit spill data that is available through the historical analysis. For example, we have spill data by pipeline diameter only for lines < and >=10", so a full spectrum of pipeline diameters would be redundant. An important aspect of the information in Table 3.3, however, is the distribution of the facilities by water depth, as there is a significant variation in pipeline Arctic hazards by water depth.

It was assumed that the facility quantities vary in accordance with a uniform distribution. Table 3.4 shows the upper and lower limits, and the base or value of each annual quantity under consideration. Thus, for example, in the year 2020, the number of on platform wells can range between 4 and 6.

Table 3.2
Summary of Exploration and Development Scenario, Chukchi Sea OCS

Scenario Element	Range	Comments
Oil production (Bbbl)	1	First development project only
Natural gas production	0	Delayed for North Slope gas line; reinjected
Exploration wells	3-6	2-5 wells are dry holes or sub-commercial shows
Delineation wells	4-8	Confirm and define the commercial discovery
Production platforms	1	Central platform with processing facility; supports 4-20 subsea satellite templates
Production wells	80-120	Total includes 20-80 subsea production wells
Service wells	20-40	All service wells are on platform
In-field flowlines (mi)	10-50	Gathering system from subsea wells
Offshore sales pipeline (mi)	30-150	Possible distance to landfall
Onshore sales pipeline (mi)	Up to 300	Connecting to existing/future North Slope pipelines
Peak production (kBpd)	200-250	Oil production only. Associated gas is reinjected
New landfall	1	Point Belcher near Wainwright
New support shorebase	1	Point Belcher near Wainwright
New processing facility	1	Co-located with shorebase
New waste facility	1	Co-located with shorebase
Drilling fluid discharge by exploration wells (tons)	665-1330	475 tons/well with 80% recycled for all expl and delin wells (95 tons discharged for 7-14 wells)
Rock cutting discharge by exploration wells (tons)	4200-8400	600 tons/well (7-14 wells total)
Discharges during development drilling	0	80% of drilling fluids are recycled; remaining waste fluids and rock cuttings for on-platform wells will be disposed of in service wells. Drilling wastes from subsea wells will be barged to an on-shore disposal facility.
Years of activity	30-40	Period from lease sale to end of oil production

Table 3.3
Chukchi Sea Development Data (2009-2044)
(App. Table 3.1)

Year	Water Depth	Well Drilling		Production Platforms		On Platform Production Wells		Subsea Production Wells		Total Production Wells		In-use Pipeline Length [miles]						Production MMbbl
												Sum<10"		Sum >=10"		Sum All		
		Exploration	Development	Incr.	Cum.	Incr.	Cum.	Incr.	Cum.	Incr.	Cum.	Incr.	Cum.	Incr.	Cum.	Incr.	Cum.	
2009	Shallow																	
	Medium																	
	Deep	1																
	Total	**1**																
2010	Shallow																	
	Medium																	
	Deep	1																
	Total	**1**																
2011	Shallow																	
	Medium																	
	Deep		2															
	Total		**2**															
2012	Shallow																	
	Medium																	
	Deep		2															
	Total		**2**															
2013	Shallow																	
	Medium																	
	Deep		2															
	Total		**2**															
2014	Shallow																	
	Medium																	
	Deep	1																
	Total	**1**																
2015	Shallow																	
	Medium																	
	Deep	1																
	Total	**1**																
2016	Shallow																	
	Medium																	
	Deep																	
	Total																	
2017	Shallow																	
	Medium																	
	Deep																	
	Total																	
2018	Shallow																	
	Medium																	
	Deep																	
	Total																	
2019	Shallow																	
	Medium																	
	Deep		6					6	6	6	6							
	Total		**6**					**6**	**6**	**6**	**6**							
2020	Shallow																	
	Medium													30	30	30	30	
	Deep		11	1	1	5	5	6	12	11	17	10	10	60	60	70	70	54.0
	Total		**11**	**1**	**1**	**5**	**5**	**6**	**12**	**11**	**17**	**10**	**10**	**90**	**90**	**100**	**100**	**54.0**

Table 3.3 ~ *Continued* ~

Year	Water Depth	Well Drilling		Production Platforms		On Platform Production Wells		Subsea Production Wells		Total Production Wells		In-use Pipeline Length [miles]						Production MMbbl
												Sum<10"		Sum >=10"		Sum All		
		Exploration	Development	Incr.	Cum.	Incr.	Cum.	Incr.	Cum.	Incr.	Cum.	Incr.	Cum.	Incr.	Cum.	Incr.	Cum.	
2021	Shallow																	
	Medium														30		30	
	Deep		21		1	15	20	6	18	21	38	5	15		60	5	75	70.0
	Total		**21**		**1**	**15**	**20**	**6**	**18**	**21**	**38**	**5**	**15**		**90**	5	105	**70.0**
2022	Shallow																	
	Medium														30		30	
	Deep		21		1	15	35	6	24	21	59	5	20		60	5	80	82.0
	Total		**21**		**1**	**15**	**35**	**6**	**24**	**21**	**59**	**5**	**20**		**90**	5	110	**82.0**
2023	Shallow																	
	Medium														30		30	
	Deep		21		1	15	50	6	30	21	80	5	25		60	5	85	82.0
	Total		**21**		**1**	**15**	**50**	**6**	**30**	**21**	**80**	**5**	**25**		**90**	5	115	**82.0**
2024	Shallow																	
	Medium														30		30	
	Deep		12		1	6	56	6	36	12	92	5	30		60	5	90	82.0
	Total		**12**		**1**	**6**	**56**	**6**	**36**	**12**	**92**	**5**	**30**		**90**	5	120	**82.0**
2025	Shallow																	
	Medium														30		30	
	Deep		6		1	6	62		36	6	98		30		60		90	82.0
	Total		**6**		**1**	**6**	**62**		**36**	**6**	**98**		**30**		**90**		120	**82.0**
2026	Shallow																	
	Medium														30		30	
	Deep				1		62		36		98		30		60		90	72.2
	Total				**1**		**62**		**36**		**98**		**30**		**90**		120	**72.2**
2027	Shallow																	
	Medium														30		30	
	Deep				1		62		36		98		30		60		90	63.5
	Total				**1**		**62**		**36**		**98**		**30**		**90**		120	**63.5**
2028	Shallow																	
	Medium														30		30	
	Deep				1		62		36		98		30		60		90	55.9
	Total				**1**		**62**		**36**		**98**		**30**		**90**		120	**55.9**
2029	Shallow																	
	Medium														30		30	
	Deep				1		62		36		98		30		60		90	49.2
	Total				**1**		**62**		**36**		**98**		**30**		**90**		120	**49.2**
2030	Shallow																	
	Medium														30		30	
	Deep				1		62		36		98		30		60		90	43.3
	Total				**1**		**62**		**36**		**98**		**30**		**90**		120	**43.3**
2031	Shallow																	
	Medium														30		30	
	Deep				1		62		36		98		30		60		90	38.1
	Total				**1**		**62**		**36**		**98**		**30**		**90**		120	**38.1**
2032	Shallow																	
	Medium														30		30	
	Deep				1		62		36		98		30		60		90	33.5
	Total				**1**		**62**		**36**		**98**		**30**		**90**		120	**33.5**
2033	Shallow																	
	Medium														30		30	
	Deep				1		62		36		98		30		60		90	29.5
	Total				**1**		**62**		**36**		**98**		**30**		**90**		120	**29.5**

Table 3.3 ~ *Continued* ~

Year	Water Depth	Well Drilling		Production Platforms		On Platform Production Wells		Subsea Production Wells		Total Production Wells		In-use Pipeline Length [miles]						Production MMbbl
												Sum<10"		Sum >=10"		Sum All		
		Exploration	Development	Incr.	Cum.	Incr.	Cum.	Incr.	Cum.	Incr.	Cum.	Incr.	Cum.	Incr.	Cum.	Incr.	Cum.	
2034	Shallow																	
	Medium														30		30	
	Deep				1		62		36		98		30		60		90	26.0
	Total				**1**		**62**		**36**		**98**		**30**		**90**		120	**26.0**
2035	Shallow																	
	Medium														30		30	
	Deep				1		62		36		98		30		60		90	22.8
	Total				**1**		**62**		**36**		**98**		**30**		**90**		120	**22.8**
2036	Shallow																	
	Medium														30		30	
	Deep				1		62		36		98		30		60		90	20.1
	Total				**1**		**62**		**36**		**98**		**30**		**90**		120	**20.1**
2037	Shallow																	
	Medium														30		30	
	Deep				1		62		36		98		30		60		90	17.7
	Total				**1**		**62**		**36**		**98**		**30**		**90**		120	**17.7**
2038	Shallow																	
	Medium														30		30	
	Deep				1		62		36		98		30		60		90	15.6
	Total				**1**		**62**		**36**		**98**		**30**		**90**		120	**15.6**
2039	Shallow																	
	Medium														30		30	
	Deep				1		62	-6	30	-6	92		30		60		90	13.7
	Total				**1**		**62**	**-6**	**30**	**-6**	**92**		**30**		**90**		120	**13.7**
2040	Shallow																	
	Medium														30		30	
	Deep				1	-5	57	-6	24	-11	81		30		60		90	12.1
	Total				**1**	**-5**	**57**	**-6**	**24**	**-11**	**81**		**30**		**90**		120	**12.1**
2041	Shallow																	
	Medium														30		30	
	Deep				1	-15	42	-6	18	-21	60		30		60		90	10.6
	Total				**1**	**-15**	**42**	**-6**	**18**	**-21**	**60**		**30**		**90**		120	**10.6**
2042	Shallow																	
	Medium														30		30	
	Deep				1	-15	27	-6	12	-21	39		30		60		90	9.3
	Total				**1**	**-15**	**27**	**-6**	**12**	**-21**	**39**		**30**		**90**		120	**9.3**
2043	Shallow																	
	Medium														30		30	
	Deep				1	-15	12	-6	6	-21	18		30		60		90	8.2
	Total				**1**	**-15**	**12**	**-6**	**6**	**-21**	**18**		**30**		**90**		120	**8.2**
2044	Shallow																	
	Medium														30		30	
	Deep				1	-6	6	-6		-12	6		30		60		90	7.2
	Total				**1**	**-6**	**6**	**-6**		**-12**	**6**		**30**		**90**		120	**7.2**

Table 3.4
Chukchi Sea Development Parameter Ranges (2009-2044)
(App. Table 3.1A)

Year	Water Depth	Well Drilling		Production Platforms	On Platform Production Wells				Subsea Production Wells				Total Production Wells				In-use Pipeline Length [miles]												Production MMbbl
		Exploration	Development	Cum.	Cum.	Range Factor		Unif. Dist. MD.	Cum.	Range Factor		Unif. Dist. MD.	Cum.	Range Factor		Unif. Dist. MD.	Sum<10"				Sum >=10"				Sum All				
						0.80	1.20			0.80	1.20			0.80	1.20		Cum.	Range Factor		Unif. Dist. MD.	Cum.	Range Factor		Unif. Dist. MD.	Cum.	Range Factor		Unif. Dist MD.	
																		0.33	1.67			0.33	1.67			0.33	1.67		
2009	Shallow																												
	Medium																												
	Deep	1																											
	Total	**1**																											
2010	Shallow																												
	Medium																												
	Deep	1																											
	Total	**1**																											
2011	Shallow																												
	Medium																												
	Deep		2																										
	Total		**2**																										
2012	Shallow																												
	Medium																												
	Deep		2																										
	Total		**2**																										
2013	Shallow																												
	Medium																												
	Deep		2																										
	Total		**2**																										
2014	Shallow																												
	Medium																												
	Deep	1																											
	Total	**1**																											
2015	Shallow																												
	Medium																												
	Deep	1																											
	Total	**1**																											
2016	Shallow																												
	Medium																												
	Deep																												
	Total																												
2017	Shallow																												
	Medium																												
	Deep																												
	Total																												
2018	Shallow																												
	Medium																												
	Deep																												
	Total																												

Table 3.4 ~ *Continued* ~

Year	Water Depth	Well Drilling		Production Platforms	On Platform Production Wells				Subsea Production Wells				Total Production Wells				In-use Pipeline Length [miles]												Production MMbbl
																	Sum<10"				Sum >=10"				Sum All				
		Exploration	Development	Cum.	Cum.	Range Factor 0.80	Range Factor 1.20	Unif. Dist. MD.	Cum.	Range Factor 0.80	Range Factor 1.20	Unif. Dist. MD.	Cum.	Range Factor 0.80	Range Factor 1.20	Unif. Dist. MD.	Cum.	Range Factor 0.33	Range Factor 1.67	Unif. Dist. MD.	Cum.	Range Factor 0.33	Range Factor 1.67	Unif. Dist. MD.	Cum.	Range Factor 0.33	Range Factor 1.67	Unif. Dist. MD.	
2019	Shallow																												
	Medium																												
	Deep		6						6	5	7	6	6	5	7	6													
	Total		**6**						**6**	**5**	**7**	**6**	**6**	**5**	**7**	**6**													
2020	Shallow																												
	Medium																				30	10	50	30	30	10	50	30	
	Deep		11	1	5	4	6	5	12	10	14	12	17	14	20	17	10	3	17	10	60	20	100	60	70	23	117	70	54.0
	Total		**11**	**1**	**5**	**4**	**6**	**5**	**12**	**10**	**14**	**12**	**17**	**14**	**20**	**17**	**10**	**3**	**17**	**10**	**90**	**30**	**150**	**90**	**100**	**33**	**167**	**100**	**54.0**
2021	Shallow																												
	Medium																				30	10	50	30	30	10	50	30	
	Deep		21	1	20	16	24	20	18	14	22	18	38	30	46	38	15	5	25	15	60	20	100	60	75	25	125	75	70.0
	Total		**21**	**1**	**20**	**16**	**24**	**20**	**18**	**14**	**22**	**18**	**38**	**30**	**46**	**38**	**15**	**5**	**25**	**15**	**90**	**30**	**150**	**90**	**105**	**35**	**175**	**105**	**70.0**
2022	Shallow																												
	Medium																				30	10	50	30	30	10	50	30	
	Deep		21	1	35	28	42	35	24	19	29	24	59	47	71	59	20	7	33	20	60	20	100	60	80	26	134	80	82.0
	Total		**21**	**1**	**35**	**28**	**42**	**35**	**24**	**19**	**29**	**24**	**59**	**47**	**71**	**59**	**20**	**7**	**33**	**20**	**90**	**30**	**150**	**90**	**110**	**36**	**184**	**110**	**82.0**
2023	Shallow																												
	Medium																				30	10	50	30	30	10	50	30	
	Deep		21	1	50	40	60	50	30	24	36	30	80	64	96	80	25	8	42	25	60	20	100	60	85	28	142	85	82.0
	Total		**21**	**1**	**50**	**40**	**60**	**50**	**30**	**24**	**36**	**30**	**80**	**64**	**96**	**80**	**25**	**8**	**42**	**25**	**90**	**30**	**150**	**90**	**115**	**38**	**192**	**115**	**82.0**
2024	Shallow																												
	Medium																				30	10	50	30	30	10	50	30	
	Deep		12	1	56	45	67	56	36	29	43	36	92	74	110	92	30	10	50	30	60	20	100	60	90	30	150	90	82.0
	Total		**12**	**1**	**56**	**45**	**67**	**56**	**36**	**29**	**43**	**36**	**92**	**74**	**110**	**92**	**30**	**10**	**50**	**30**	**90**	**30**	**150**	**90**	**120**	**40**	**200**	**120**	**82.0**
2025	Shallow																												
	Medium																				30	10	50	30	30	10	50	30	
	Deep		6	1	62	50	74	62	36	29	43	36	98	78	118	98	30	10	50	30	60	20	100	60	90	30	150	90	82.0
	Total		**6**	**1**	**62**	**50**	**74**	**62**	**36**	**29**	**43**	**36**	**98**	**78**	**118**	**98**	**30**	**10**	**50**	**30**	**90**	**30**	**150**	**90**	**120**	**40**	**200**	**120**	**82.0**
2026	Shallow																												
	Medium																				30	10	50	30	30	10	50	30	
	Deep			1	62	50	74	62	36	29	43	36	98	78	118	98	30	10	50	30	60	20	100	60	90	30	150	90	72.2
	Total			**1**	**62**	**50**	**74**	**62**	**36**	**29**	**43**	**36**	**98**	**78**	**118**	**98**	**30**	**10**	**50**	**30**	**90**	**30**	**150**	**90**	**120**	**40**	**200**	**120**	**72.2**
2027	Shallow																												
	Medium																				30	10	50	30	30	10	50	30	
	Deep			1	62	50	74	62	36	29	43	36	98	78	118	98	30	10	50	30	60	20	100	60	90	30	150	90	63.5
	Total			**1**	**62**	**50**	**74**	**62**	**36**	**29**	**43**	**36**	**98**	**78**	**118**	**98**	**30**	**10**	**50**	**30**	**90**	**30**	**150**	**90**	**120**	**40**	**200**	**120**	**63.5**
2028	Shallow																												
	Medium																				30	10	50	30	30	10	50	30	
	Deep			1	62	50	74	62	36	29	43	36	98	78	118	98	30	10	50	30	60	20	100	60	90	30	150	90	55.9
	Total			**1**	**62**	**50**	**74**	**62**	**36**	**29**	**43**	**36**	**98**	**78**	**118**	**98**	**30**	**10**	**50**	**30**	**90**	**30**	**150**	**90**	**120**	**40**	**200**	**120**	**55.9**
2029	Shallow																												
	Medium																				30	10	50	30	30	10	50	30	
	Deep			1	62	50	74	62	36	29	43	36	98	78	118	98	30	10	50	30	60	20	100	60	90	30	150	90	49.2
	Total			**1**	**62**	**50**	**74**	**62**	**36**	**29**	**43**	**36**	**98**	**78**	**118**	**98**	**30**	**10**	**50**	**30**	**90**	**30**	**150**	**90**	**120**	**40**	**200**	**120**	**49.2**
2030	Shallow																												

Table 3.4 ~ *Continued* ~

Year	Water Depth	Well Drilling		Production Platforms	On Platform Production Wells				Subsea Production Wells				Total Production Wells				In-use Pipeline Length [miles]												Production MMbbl
																	Sum<10"				Sum >=10"				Sum All				
						Range Factor				Range Factor				Range Factor				Range Factor				Range Factor				Range Factor			
		Exploration	Development	Cum.	Cum.	0.80	1.20	Unif. Dist. MD.	Cum.	0.80	1.20	Unif. Dist. MD.	Cum.	0.80	1.20	Unif. Dist. MD.	Cum.	0.33	1.67	Unif. Dist. MD.	Cum.	0.33	1.67	Unif. Dist. MD.	Cum.	0.33	1.67	Unif. Dist. MD.	
	Medium																				30	10	50	30	30	10	50	30	
	Deep			1	62	50	74	62	36	29	43	36	98	78	118	98	30	10	50	30	60	20	100	60	90	30	150	90	43.3
	Total			**1**	**62**	**50**	**74**	**62**	**36**	**29**	**43**	**36**	**98**	**78**	**118**	**98**	**30**	**10**	**50**	**30**	**90**	**30**	**150**	**90**	**120**	**40**	**200**	**120**	**43.3**
2031	Shallow																												
	Medium																				30	10	50	30	30	10	50	30	
	Deep			1	62	50	74	62	36	29	43	36	98	78	118	98	30	10	50	30	60	20	100	60	90	30	150	90	38.1
	Total			**1**	**62**	**50**	**74**	**62**	**36**	**29**	**43**	**36**	**98**	**78**	**118**	**98**	**30**	**10**	**50**	**30**	**90**	**30**	**150**	**90**	**120**	**40**	**200**	**120**	**38.1**
2032	Shallow																												
	Medium																				30	10	50	30	30	10	50	30	
	Deep			1	62	50	74	62	36	29	43	36	98	78	118	98	30	10	50	30	60	20	100	60	90	30	150	90	33.5
	Total			**1**	**62**	**50**	**74**	**62**	**36**	**29**	**43**	**36**	**98**	**78**	**118**	**98**	**30**	**10**	**50**	**30**	**90**	**30**	**150**	**90**	**120**	**40**	**200**	**120**	**33.5**
2033	Shallow																												
	Medium																				30	10	50	30	30	10	50	30	
	Deep			1	62	50	74	62	36	29	43	36	98	78	118	98	30	10	50	30	60	20	100	60	90	30	150	90	29.5
	Total			**1**	**62**	**50**	**74**	**62**	**36**	**29**	**43**	**36**	**98**	**78**	**118**	**98**	**30**	**10**	**50**	**30**	**90**	**30**	**150**	**90**	**120**	**40**	**200**	**120**	**29.5**
2034	Shallow																												
	Medium																				30	10	50	30	30	10	50	30	
	Deep			1	62	50	74	62	36	29	43	36	98	78	118	98	30	10	50	30	60	20	100	60	90	30	150	90	26.0
	Total			**1**	**62**	**50**	**74**	**62**	**36**	**29**	**43**	**36**	**98**	**78**	**118**	**98**	**30**	**10**	**50**	**30**	**90**	**30**	**150**	**90**	**120**	**40**	**200**	**120**	**26.0**
2035	Shallow																												
	Medium																				30	10	50	30	30	10	50	30	
	Deep			1	62	50	74	62	36	29	43	36	98	78	118	98	30	10	50	30	60	20	100	60	90	30	150	90	22.8
	Total			**1**	**62**	**50**	**74**	**62**	**36**	**29**	**43**	**36**	**98**	**78**	**118**	**98**	**30**	**10**	**50**	**30**	**90**	**30**	**150**	**90**	**120**	**40**	**200**	**120**	**22.8**
2036	Shallow																												
	Medium																				30	10	50	30	30	10	50	30	
	Deep			1	62	50	74	62	36	29	43	36	98	78	118	98	30	10	50	30	60	20	100	60	90	30	150	90	20.1
	Total			**1**	**62**	**50**	**74**	**62**	**36**	**29**	**43**	**36**	**98**	**78**	**118**	**98**	**30**	**10**	**50**	**30**	**90**	**30**	**150**	**90**	**120**	**40**	**200**	**120**	**20.1**
2037	Shallow																												
	Medium																				30	10	50	30	30	10	50	30	
	Deep			1	62	50	74	62	36	29	43	36	98	78	118	98	30	10	50	30	60	20	100	60	90	30	150	90	17.7
	Total			**1**	**62**	**50**	**74**	**62**	**36**	**29**	**43**	**36**	**98**	**78**	**118**	**98**	**30**	**10**	**50**	**30**	**90**	**30**	**150**	**90**	**120**	**40**	**200**	**120**	**17.7**
2038	Shallow																												
	Medium																				30	10	50	30	30	10	50	30	
	Deep			1	62	50	74	62	36	29	43	36	98	78	118	98	30	10	50	30	60	20	100	60	90	30	150	90	15.6
	Total			**1**	**62**	**50**	**74**	**62**	**36**	**29**	**43**	**36**	**98**	**78**	**118**	**98**	**30**	**10**	**50**	**30**	**90**	**30**	**150**	**90**	**120**	**40**	**200**	**120**	**15.6**
2039	Shallow																												
	Medium																				30	10	50	30	30	10	50	30	
	Deep			1	62	50	74	62	30	24	36	30	92	74	110	92	30	10	50	30	60	20	100	60	90	30	150	90	13.7
	Total			**1**	**62**	**50**	**74**	**62**	**30**	**24**	**36**	**30**	**92**	**74**	**110**	**92**	**30**	**10**	**50**	**30**	**90**	**30**	**150**	**90**	**120**	**40**	**200**	**120**	**13.7**
2040	Shallow																												
	Medium																				30	10	50	30	30	10	50	30	
	Deep			1	57	46	68	57	24	19	29	24	81	65	97	81	30	10	50	30	60	20	100	60	90	30	150	90	12.1
	Total			**1**	**57**	**46**	**68**	**57**	**24**	**19**	**29**	**24**	**81**	**65**	**97**	**81**	**30**	**10**	**50**	**30**	**90**	**30**	**150**	**90**	**120**	**40**	**200**	**120**	**12.1**
2041	Shallow																												
	Medium																				30	10	50	30	30	10	50	30	
	Deep			1	42	34	50	42	18	14	22	18	60	48	72	60	30	10	50	30	60	20	100	60	90	30	150	90	10.6

Table 3.4 ~ *Continued* ~

Year	Water Depth	Well Drilling		Production Platforms	On Platform Production Wells				Subsea Production Wells				Total Production Wells				In-use Pipeline Length [miles]												Production MMbbl
																	Sum<10"				Sum >=10"				Sum All				
						Range Factor				Range Factor				Range Factor				Range Factor				Range Factor				Range Factor			
		Exploration	Development	Cum.	Cum.	0.80	1.20	Unif. Dist. MD.	Cum.	0.80	1.20	Unif. Dist. MD.	Cum.	0.80	1.20	Unif. Dist. MD.	Cum.	0.33	1.67	Unif. Dist. MD.	Cum.	0.33	1.67	Unif. Dist. MD.	Cum.	0.33	1.67	Unif. Dist. MD.	
	Total			1	42	34	50	42	18	14	22	18	60	48	72	60	30	10	50	30	90	30	150	90	120	40	200	120	10.6
2042	Shallow																												
	Medium																				30	10	50	30	30	10	50	30	
	Deep			1	27	22	32	27	12	10	14	12	39	31	47	39	30	10	50	30	60	20	100	60	90	30	150	90	9.3
	Total			1	27	22	32	27	12	10	14	12	39	31	47	39	30	10	50	30	90	30	150	90	120	40	200	120	9.3
2043	Shallow																												
	Medium																				30	10	50	30	30	10	50	30	
	Deep			1	12	10	14	12	6	5	7	6	18	14	22	18	30	10	50	30	60	20	100	60	90	30	150	90	8.2
	Total			1	12	10	14	12	6	5	7	6	18	14	22	18	30	10	50	30	90	30	150	90	120	40	200	120	8.2
2044	Shallow																												
	Medium																				30	10	50	30	30	10	50	30	
	Deep			1	6	5	7	6					6	5	7	6	30	10	50	30	60	20	100	60	90	30	150	90	7.2
	Total			1	6	5	7	6					6	5	7	6	30	10	50	30	90	30	150	90	120	40	200	120	7.2

CHAPTER 4

FAULT TREE ANALYSIS FOR ARCTIC OIL SPILL FREQUENCIES

4.1 General Description of Fault Tree Analysis

Fault trees are a method for modeling the occurrence of failures. They are used when an adequate history to provide failure statistics is not available. Developed initially by Rasmussen for the US Nuclear Regulatory Commission in the early 1970s [65, 51], fault trees have become a popular risk analytic tool for predicting risks, assessing relative risks, and quantifying comparative risks [7, 9, 14, 15, 18, 23, 26, 45]. In 1976, we first used fault trees to quantify oil spill probabilities in the Canadian Beaufort Sea for the Canadian Department of the Environment [10, 11]. In the present study they are used for the transformation of historical oil spill statistics for non-Arctic regions to predictive oil spill statistics for Arctic regions in the study area.

4.2 Fault Tree Methodology

4.2.1 Fault Tree Analysis Basics

The basic symbols used in the graphic depiction of simple (as used here) fault tree networks are illustrated in Figure 4.1(a). As may be seen, the two types of symbols designate logic gates and event types. The basic fault tree building blocks are the events and associated sub-events, which form a causal network. The elements linking events are the AND and OR gates, which define the logical relationship among events in the network. The output event from an OR gate occurs if any one or more of the input events to the gate occurs. The output event from an AND gate occurs only if all the input events occur simultaneously.

The basic structure of a fault tree is illustrated in Figure 4.1(b). Because of their connection through an AND gate, Event D and Event E must both occur for the resultant Event B to occur. An OR gate connects Events B and C; therefore, the occurrence of either one or both of Events B and C results in the occurrence of the resultant Event A. As may be seen, the principal fault tree structures are easy to apply; however, the representation of complex problems often requires very large fault trees, which become more difficult to analyze and require more advanced techniques such as minimal cut-set analysis [2, 14, 18, 23, 51]. For the present application, a simple system connected through OR gates only will used.

SYMBOL	DESCRIPTION
A. LOGIC	
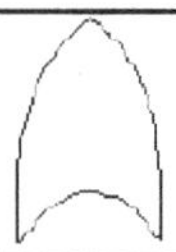	EITHER / OR GATE
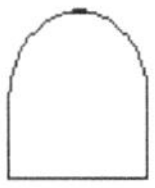	AND GATE
B. EVENT	
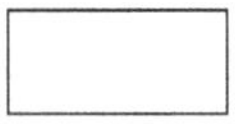	RESULTANT EVENT
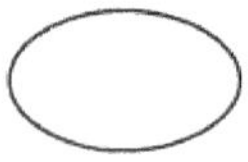	BASIC EVENT

(a) Basic Fault Tree Symbols

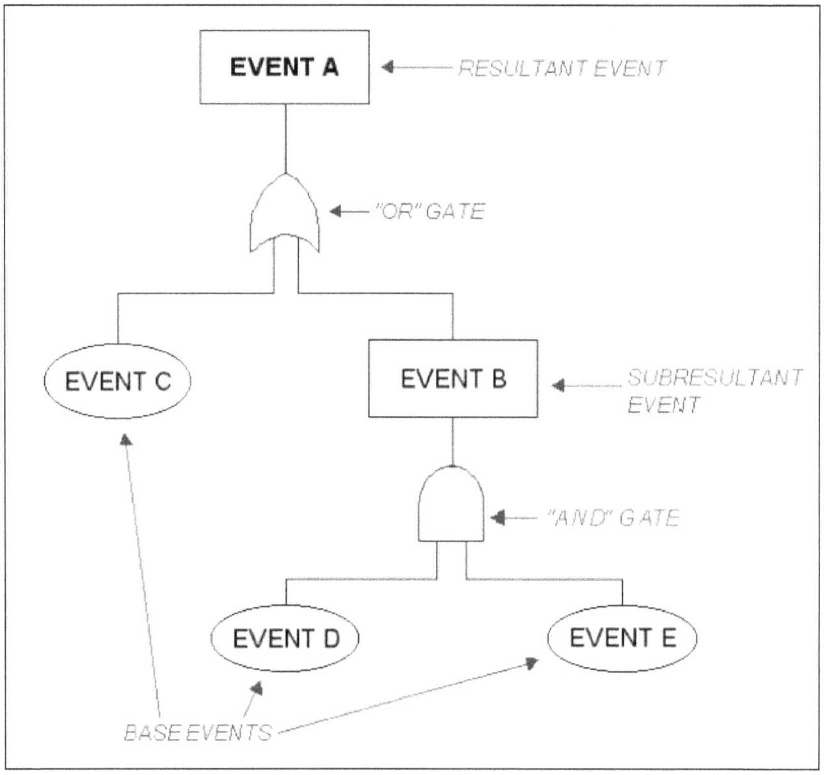

(b) Basic Fault Tree Structure

Figure 4.1
Fault Tree Basics

Computationally, the probability of input events joined through an AND gate are multiplied to calculate the probabilities of the output event. The probabilities of input events joined through an OR gate are added to calculate the probability of the output event. The relevant equations and associated assumptions may be summarized as follows:

For AND Gate:

$$P = \prod_{n}^{i=1} P_i \tag{4.1a}$$

Example: Output Event Probability = P_x
Input Events failure probabilities, P_1, P_2, ...

$$P_x = P_1(P_2)(P_3) \tag{4.1b}$$

For OR Gate:

$$P = 1 - \prod_{n}^{i=1}(1 - P_i) \tag{4.2a}$$

Example: Output Event Probability = P_y
Input Event failure probabilities, P_1, P_2, ...

$$P_y = 1 - \prod_{n}(1 - P_1)(1 - P_2)(1 - P_3)$$

$$P_y = P_1 + P_2 + P_3; \; for \; P_i \leq 0.1 \tag{4.2b}$$

In more complex fault trees, it is necessary to assure that base events which affect more than one fault tree branch are not numerically duplicated. This is done through the use of minimal cut-set theory [14, 18, 23, 51]. However, as indicated earlier, the fault trees used in this study are sufficiently simple in structure and level of detail to exclude the requirement of using minimal cut-set theory in their computation algorithms.

4.2.2 Current Application of Fault Trees

Figure 4.2 illustrates a two-tier fault tree that can be used to develop pipeline large spill frequencies for the Arctic study area from the historical frequencies. Note that this example is illustrative of the process only, and does not correspond to the same numerical values used in computations later. The type of fault tree shown, to be used extensively later, is a relatively simple fault tree showing the resultant event, the spill, generated from a series of subresultant events corresponding to the pipeline spill causal classification, such as that shown in Table 2.3. The upper tier of numbers (marked "H") below each of the events in the fault tree represents the historical frequency (per 100,000 km-yr) while the lower one (marked "A") represents the modified frequency for Arctic operations. As these fault trees are composed entirely of OR gates, the computation of resultant events is quite simple – consisting of the addition of the probabilities of events at each level of the fault tree to obtain the resultant probability at the next higher value.

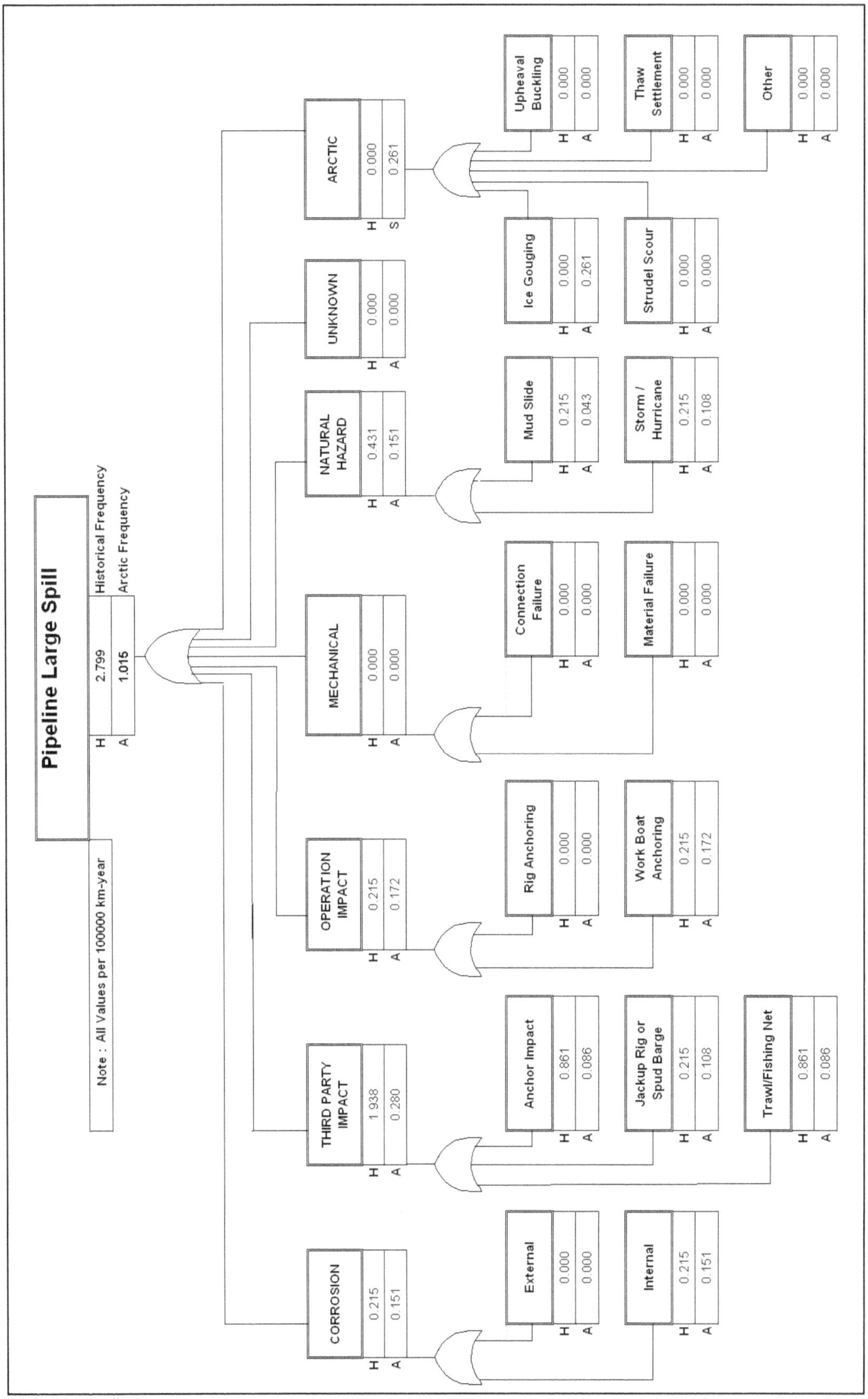

Figure 4.2
Example of Fault Tree to Transform Historical (GOM) to Arctic Spill Frequencies[1]

[1] The input data used here are only illustrative and do not represent the inputs used later in this study.

For example, to obtain the "Natural Hazard" Arctic ("A") probability of 0.151, add 0.043 and 0.108. Essentially, the fault tree resultant (top event) shows that the Arctic frequency of spills (for the example pipeline category, location, and spill size) is approximately 1 in 100,000 km-yr or 1.015 x 10^{-5}/km-yr. The non-Arctic historical frequency for this spill size, by comparison, is 2.799 x 10^{-5}/km-yr, or approximately 2.8 times higher. Both frequencies are for illustrative purposes only.

4.2.3 Monte Carlo Simulation

A type of numerical simulation, called Monte Carlo simulation [9] can be used to obtain the outcome of a set of interactions for equations in which the independent variables are described by distributions of any arbitrary form. The Monte Carlo simulation is a systematic method for selecting values from each of the independent variable distributions and computing all valid combinations of these values to obtain the distribution of the dependent variable. Naturally, this is done utilizing a computer, so that thousands of combinations can be rapidly computed and assembled to give the output distribution.

Consider the example of the following equation:

$$X = X_1 + X_2 \qquad \textbf{(4.3)}$$

Where X is the dependent variable (such as the resultant spill frequency) and X_1 and X_2 are base event probabilities joined through an "and" gate. Suppose now that X_1 and X_2 are some arbitrary distributions that can be described by a collection of values x_1 and x_2. What we do in the Monte Carlo process, figuratively, is to put the collection of the X_1 values into one hat, the X_1 hat, and the same for the X_2 values – into an X_2 hat. We then randomly draw one value from each of the hats and compute the resultant value of the dependent variable, X, using equation 4.3. This is done several thousand times. Thus, a resultant or dependent variable distribution, X, is estimated from the computations of all valid combinations of the independent variables (X_1 and X_2).

Generally, the resultant can be viewed as a cumulative distribution function as illustrated in Figure 4.3. Such a cumulative distribution function (CDF) is also a measure of the accuracy or, conversely, the variance of the distribution. As can be seen from this figure, if the distribution is a vertical line, no matter where one draws on the vertical axis, the same value of the variable will result – that is, the variable is a constant. At the other extreme, if the variable is completely random then the distribution will be represented as a diagonal straight line between the minimum and maximum value. Intermediate qualitative descriptions of the randomness of the variable follow from inspection of the CDF in Figure 4.3.

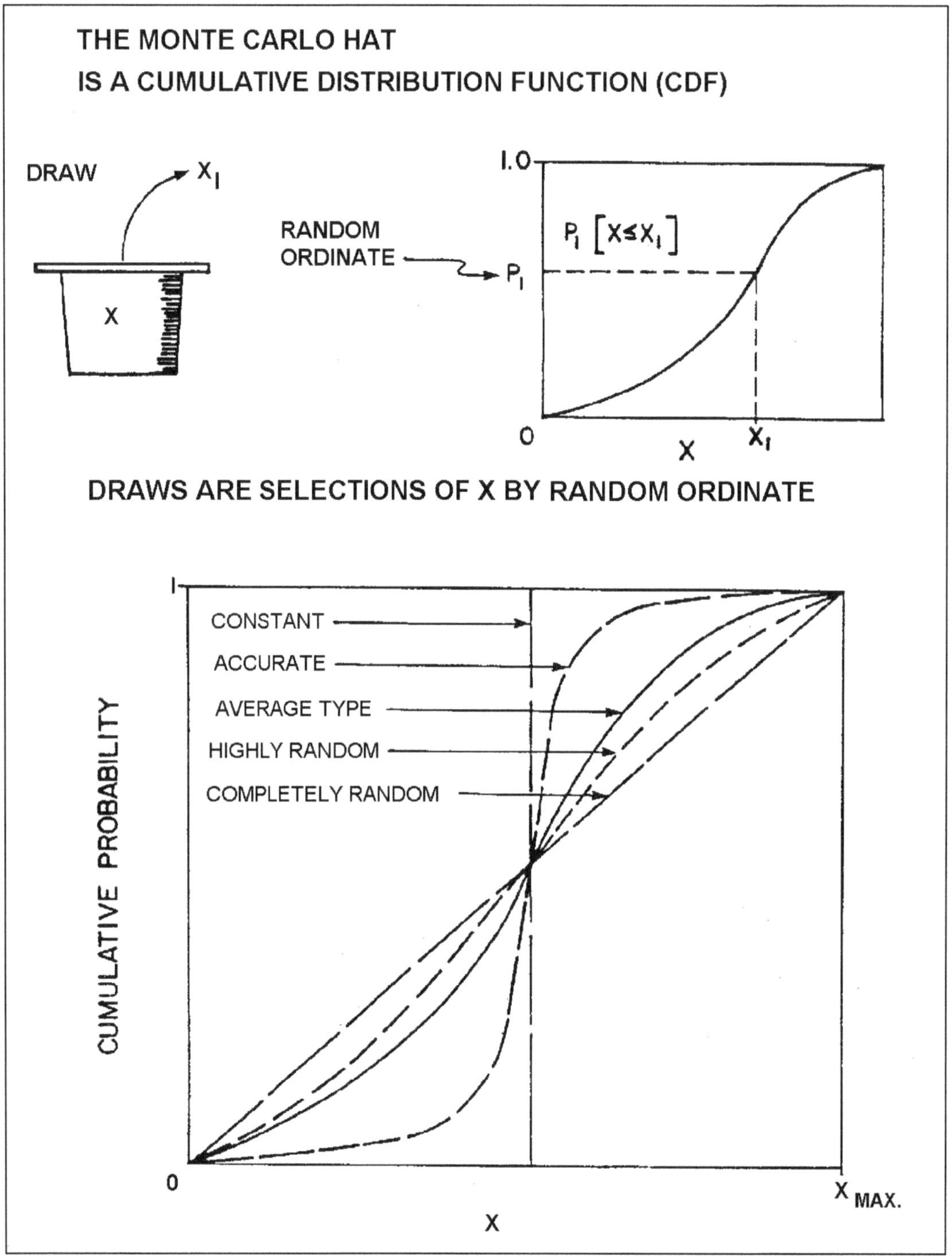
THE MONTE CARLO HAT
IS A CUMULATIVE DISTRIBUTION FUNCTION (CDF)
DRAW
X
RANDOM ORDINATE
1.0
P [X≤X]
P
0
X
DRAWS ARE SELECTIONS OF X BY RANDOM ORDINATE
CONSTANT
ACCURATE
AVERAGE TYPE
HIGHLY RANDOM
COMPLETELY RANDOM
CUMULATIVE PROBABILITY
0
X
X MAX.

Figure 4.3
Monte Carlo Technique Schematic

There are two other important concepts related to the CDF enter into Monte Carlo modeling: auto-correlation and cross-correlation. Suppose the variables X_1 can vary only within a specified interval over the simulation time increment. Then, after the first random draw, the next draw would be restricted within certain limits of the initial draw simply as a result of the physical restrictions of the problem. Such a restriction is represented as an auto-correlation coefficient. Now, suppose that not only are the X_1 restricted, but also the X_2. Suppose further, however, that given a certain X_1, a restriction were placed on the range of X_2 associated with that X_1. Say, only small X_1 could associate with the full range of X_2, while large X_1 could only be associated with certain lower X_2. Then, such a relationship would be expressed as a cross-correlation factor and certain limits would be imposed for the drawing on both X_1 and associated X_2. In the present analysis, all distributed variables are considered to be independent – so that auto and cross-correlations need not be invoked.

4.2.4 Distribution Derived from Historical Data for Monte Carlo Analysis

In order to model the variability of the base data and its distribution through the Arctic effects, using the Monte Carlo approach, an appropriate distribution needs to be derived. As in the previous study [12], a Triangular Distribution was selected.

According to [13], the Triangular Distribution is typically used as a descriptor of a population for which there is only limited sample data, as is the current case. The distribution is based on a knowledge of a minimum and maximum, which was derived from the historical data here, and an educated guess as to what the modal value might be. Here, the modal value was chosen to be a function of the average historical value, as given in Equation 2.1. Despite being a simplistic description of a population, the Triangular Distribution is a very useful one for modeling processes where the relationship between variables is understood, but data are scarce.

Also, when combining several variables in a functional relationship utilizing numerical methods, as is done in Monte Carlo Simulation, the Triangular Distribution is a preferred one due to its simplicity and relatively accurate probabilistic resultant when evaluated by a large number of random draws, as occurs in the Monte Carlo process. The data used here typifies sparse data with a preferred or modal value and an easily identifiable maximum and minimum. Then, for the case of the simple upper and lower 100% confidence interval (called High and Low), the expected value ***E*** (or mean value) of the Triangular Distribution can be expressed as:

$$E = (High + Mode + Low) / 3 \qquad \textbf{(4.4)}$$

For maximum and minimum which are not at the 100% confidence interval level – such as those at 90% confidence levels – a Monte Carlo computation is used to evaluate the expected value of each distribution, giving results somewhat different from Equation 4.4. Based on the historical data earlier presented in Tables 2.4, 2.7, and 2.10, the Triangular Distribution expected value computed from the low, mode, and high values at 90% confidence intervals are given in Tables 4.1, 4.2, and 4.3, for pipelines, platforms, and wells respectively. The high and low values were calculated as described in Section 2.2.

Table 4.1
Pipeline Spill Frequency Triangular Distribution Properties
(App. Table 1.4)

GOM OCS Pipeline Spills, Categorized 1972-99		Low Factor	High Factor	Frequency spill per 10^5 km-years				
				Historical	Low	Mode	High	Expected
By Diameter, By Spill Size								
<10"	Small	0	2.57	3.7974	0	1.6329	9.7592	5.1720
	Medium	0	2.57	6.6454	0	2.8575	17.0786	9.0510
	Large	0	2.57	3.7974	0	1.6329	9.7592	5.1720
	Huge	0	2.57	0.9493	0	0.4082	2.4398	1.2930
=>10"	Small	0	2.57	2.4436	0	1.0507	6.2800	3.3282
	Medium	0	2.57	6.1090	0	2.6269	15.7001	8.3205
	Large	0	2.57	7.3308	0	3.1522	18.8401	9.9846
	Huge	0	2.57	2.4436	0	1.0507	6.2800	3.3282

Table 4.2
Platform Spill Frequency Triangular Distribution Properties
(App. Table 1.7)

Spill Size	Frequency Unit	Low Factor	High Factor	Historical	Low	Mode	High	Expected
Small and Medium Spills 50-999 bbl	spill per 10^4 well-year	0	2.88	1.5036	0.0000	0.1804	4.3303	2.1571
Large and Huge Spills =>1000 bbl	spill per 10^4 well-year	0	2.88	0.2506	0.0000	0.0301	0.7217	0.3595

Table 4.3
Well Blowout Frequency Triangular Distribution Properties
(App. Table 1.9)

EVENT	FREQUENCY UNIT	Low Factor	High Factor	Frequencies				
				Historical	Low	Mode	High	Expected
				Small and Medium Spills 50-999 bbl				
PRODUCTION WELL	spill per 10^4 well-year	0.448	1.545	0.147	0.066	0.148	0.227	0.147
EXPLORATION WELL DRILLING	spill per 10^4 wells	0.439	2.036	1.966	0.863	1.032	4.002	2.262
DEVELOPMENT WELL DRILLING	spill per 10^4 wells	0.437	1.760	0.654	0.286	0.526	1.151	0.692
				Large Spills 1000-9999 bbl				
PRODUCTION WELL	spill per 10^4 well-year	0.448	1.545	1.028	0.460	1.037	1.588	1.026
EXPLORATION WELL DRILLING	spill per 10^4 wells	0.439	2.036	13.754	6.039	7.220	28.001	15.824
DEVELOPMENT WELL DRILLING	spill per 10^4 wells	0.437	1.760	4.570	1.998	3.671	8.041	4.833
				Small, Medium and Large Spills 50-9999 bbl				
PRODUCTION WELL	spill per 10^4 well-year	0.448	1.545	1.175	0.526	1.185	1.815	1.173
EXPLORATION WELL DRILLING	spill per 10^4 wells	0.439	2.036	15.719	6.903	8.252	32.003	18.086
DEVELOPMENT WELL DRILLING	spill per 10^4 wells	0.437	1.760	5.224	2.284	4.197	9.192	5.525
				Spill 10000-149999 bbl				
PRODUCTION WELL	spill per 10^4 well-year	0.448	1.545	0.441	0.197	0.444	0.681	0.440
EXPLORATION WELL DRILLING	spill per 10^4 wells	0.439	2.036	5.909	2.595	3.102	12.031	6.799
DEVELOPMENT WELL DRILLING	spill per 10^4 wells	0.437	1.760	1.963	0.858	1.577	3.454	2.076
				Spill =>150000 bbl				
PRODUCTION WELL	spill per 10^4 well-year	0.448	1.545	0.294	0.132	0.296	0.454	0.293
EXPLORATION WELL DRILLING	spill per 10^4 wells	0.439	2.036	3.421	1.502	1.796	6.965	3.936
DEVELOPMENT WELL DRILLING	spill per 10^4 wells	0.437	1.760	1.963	0.858	1.577	3.454	2.076

4.2.5 Approaches to Assessment of Arctic Spill Frequency Variability

The method for assessment of Arctic spill frequency variability consists of systematically perturbing the variability of all the causal events, plus that of the Arctic unique effects. In this approach, the non-Arctic variable distribution is multiplied by an adjustment or correction distribution to obtain the Arctic variable distribution.

4.3 Pipeline Fault Tree Analysis

4.3.1 Arctic Pipeline Spill Causal Frequency Distributions

The effects of the Arctic environment and operations are reflected in the effect on facility failure rates in two ways; namely, through "Modified Effects", those changing the frequency component of certain fault contributions such as anchor impacts which are common to both Arctic and temperate zones, and through "Unique Effects" or additive elements such as ice gouging which are unique to the Arctic offshore environment. Table 4.4 shows the frequency modifications (in %) and frequency increment additions (per 10^5 km-yr)developed for Arctic pipelines for different spill sizes throughout the three relevant water depth ranges. The right hand column of the table gives a summary of the reasoning behind the effects. For the Arctic unique effects, both the expected value (from Table 2.9) and the median value, determined through the Monte Carlo analysis, are given. The median values differ from the expected values due to skewness of the distributions introduced through the assigned values of the upper and lower bounds (Table 2.9). The following comments can be made for each of the causes described:

- *External corrosion* – Due to the low temperature, limited biological and lowered chemical effects are expected. Coatings will be state of art and high level of quality control will be used during pipeline installation resulting in high integrity levels of coating to prevent external corrosion.
- *Internal corrosion* – Additional (above historical levels) inspection or smart pigging is anticipated.
- *Anchor impact* – The very low traffic densities of third party shipping in the area justify a 50% reduction in anchor impact expectations on the pipeline.
- *Jack-up rig or spud barges* – Associated or other operations are going to be substantially more limited than they are in the historical data population in the Gulf of Mexico.
- *Trawl/Fishing net* – Very limited fishing is expected in the Chukchi Sea.

Table 4.4
Pipeline Arctic Effect Derivation Summary
(App. Table 2.1)

CAUSE CLASSIFICATION	Spill Size	Shallow	Medium	Deep	Reason
		Historical Expected Frequency Change %			
CORROSION					
External	All	(30)	(30)	(30)	Low temperature and bio effects. Extra smart pigging.
Internal	All	(30)	(30)	(30)	Extra smart pigging.
THIRD PARTY IMPACT					
Anchor Impact	All	(50)	(50)	(50)	Low traffic.
Jackup Rig or Spud Barge	All	(50)	(50)	(50)	Low facility density.
Trawl/Fishing Net	All	(50)	(60)	(70)	Low fishing activity. Less bottom fishing in deeper water.
OPERATION IMPACT					
Rig Anchoring	All	(20)	(20)	(20)	Low marine traffic during ice season (8 months).
Work Boat Anchoring	All	(20)	(20)	(20)	Low work boat traffic during ice season (8 months).
MECHANICAL					
Connection Failure	All				
Material Failure	All				
NATURAL HAZARD					
Mud Slide	All	(60)	(50)	(40)	Gradient low. Mud slide potential (gradient) increases with water depth.
Storm/ Hurricane	All	(50)	(50)	(50)	Fewer severe storms.
		Freq. Increment per 10^5 km-year			
		Expected / Mode	Expected / Mode	Expected / Mode	
ARCTIC					
Ice Gouging	S	0.3495	0.2796		Ice gouge failure rate calculated using exponential failure distribution for 2.5-m cover, 0.2-m average gouge depth, 2 gouges per km-yr flux. Spill size Distribution explained in text Section 2.5.2. Medium depth has 0.8 as many gouges as shallow.
		0.0680	0.0544		
	M	0.6178	0.4943		
		0.1210	0.0968		
	L	1.3438	1.0750		
		0.2610	0.2088		
	H	0.3762	0.3010		
		0.0730	0.0584		
Strudel Scour	S	0.0021			Only in shallow water. Average frequency of 4 scours/mile² and 100 ft of bridge length with 10% conditional Pipelines failure probability. The same spill size distribution as above.
		0.0012			
	M	0.0038			
		0.0020			
	L	0.0082			
		0.0045			
	H	0.0023			
		0.0012			
Upheaval Buckling	S	0.0004	0.0004	0.0004	All water depth. The failure frequency is 20% of that of Strudel Scour.
		0.0002	0.0002	0.0002	
	M	0.0008	0.0008	0.0008	
		0.0004	0.0004	0.0004	
	L	0.0016	0.0016	0.0016	
		0.0009	0.0009	0.0009	
	H	0.0005	0.0005	0.0005	
		0.0002	0.0002	0.0002	
Thaw Settlement	S	0.0002	0.0002	0.0002	All water depth. The failure frequency is 10% of that of Strudel Scour.
		0.0001	0.0001	0.0001	
	M	0.0004	0.0004	0.0004	
		0.0002	0.0002	0.0002	
	L	0.0008	0.0008	0.0008	
		0.0004	0.0004	0.0004	
	H	0.0002	0.0002	0.0002	
		0.0001	0.0001	0.0001	
Other	S	0.0881	0.0701	0.0002	25% of sum of above.
		0.0174	0.0137	0.0001	
	M	0.1557	0.1238	0.0003	
		0.0309	0.0244	0.0002	
	L	0.3386	0.2694	0.0006	
		0.0667	0.0525	0.0003	
	H	0.0948	0.0754	0.0002	
		0.0187	0.0147	0.0001	

- *Rig anchoring* – Although it is anticipated that no marine traffic except possibly icebreakers will occur during the ice season, an increased traffic density during the four month open water season to resupply the platforms is expected, justifying only a 20% decrease in this failure cause.
- *Workboat anchoring* – The same applies to workboat anchoring as to rig anchoring.
- *Mechanical connection failure or material failure* – No change was made to account for Arctic effects.
- *Mudslide* – A relatively low gradient resulting in limited mudslide potential is anticipated. A gradual increase in the mudslide potential (reflected by smaller decreases in failure frequency) ranging from 60% for shallow water to only 40% in deep water was included to account for the anticipated increase in gradient as deeper waters are encountered.
- *Storms* – Considerably fewer severe storms are anticipated on an annual basis in the Arctic than in GOM, due to damping of the ocean surface by ice cover.
- *Arctic effects* – Arctic effects are effects which are unique to the Arctic and are not reflected in the historical fault tree itself. Arctic effects were discussed in detail in Chapter 2, Section 2.5. The discussion in that section is summarized in the right hand column of Table 4.4. The frequency increments in this table are given as both the "mode" values and the "expected" values. The mode values are the mode values given in Table 2.11. The expected values, however, are those calculated using the Monte Carlo method with the low, mode, and high values from Table 2.11, as inputs to the Monte Carlo. The expected or mean values are clearly considerably higher than the mode or most likely values. This lack of coincidence between expected and mode values is due to the skewness of the distribution.

Derivation of the Arctic effect distributions is accomplished through the construction of a secondary triangular distribution by which the historical causal frequency distributions are multiplied to provide the resultant Arctic effect distribution. This secondary distribution utilizes the value of mode adjustments from Table 4.4, with appropriate second order perturbations for the upper and lower 90% confidence interval bounds. Table 4.5 summarizes these Arctic effect distributions. For the Arctic modified effects, given in the top of the table, the secondary distribution is simply the frequency change used as the mode of the distribution, and 90% upper and lower confidence interval changes given under the Min and Max columns. For the Arctic unique effects, total frequency increments are given, with the upper confidence interval value at approximately 12 times the mode, and the lower bound value at approximately $^1/_{10}$ of the modal value.

Table 4.5
Pipeline Arctic Effect Distribution Derivation Summary
(App. Table 2.2)

CAUSE CLASSIFICATION	Spill Size	Shallow			Medium			Deep		
		Frequency Change %								
		Min	Mode	Max	Min	Mode	Max	Min	Mode	Max
CORROSION										
External	All	(90)	(30)	(10)	(90)	(30)	(10)	(90)	(30)	(10)
Internal	All	(90)	(30)	(10)	(90)	(30)	(10)	(90)	(30)	(10)
THIRD PARTY IMPACT										
Anchor Impact	All	(90)	(50)	(10)	(90)	(50)	(10)	(90)	(50)	(10)
Jackup Rig or Spud Barge	All	(90)	(50)	(10)	(90)	(50)	(10)	(90)	(50)	(10)
Trawl/Fishing Net	All	(90)	(50)	(10)	(90)	(60)	(10)	(90)	(70)	(10)
OPERATION IMPACT										
Rig Anchoring	All	(50)	(20)	(10)	(50)	(20)	(10)	(50)	(20)	(10)
Work Boat Anchoring	All	(50)	(20)	(10)	(50)	(20)	(10)	(50)	(20)	(10)
MECHANICAL										
Connection Failure	All									
Material Failure	All									
NATURAL HAZARD										
Mud Slide	All	(90)	(60)	(10)	(90)	(50)	(10)	(90)	(40)	(10)
Storm/ Hurricane	All	(90)	(50)	(10)	(90)	(50)	(10)	(90)	(50)	(10)
		Frequency Increment per 10^5 km-year								
ARCTIC										
Ice Gouging	S	0.0060	0.0680	0.8290	0.0048	0.0544	0.6632			
	M	0.0090	0.1210	1.4670	0.0072	0.0968	1.1736			
	L	0.0210	0.2610	3.1900	0.0168	0.2088	2.5520			
	H	0.0060	0.0730	0.8930	0.0048	0.0584	0.7144			
Strudel Scour	S	0.0004	0.0012	0.0044						
	M	0.0006	0.0020	0.0078						
	L	0.0014	0.0045	0.0170						
	H	0.0004	0.0012	0.0048						
Upheaval Buckling	S	0.00007	0.00023	0.00088	0.00007	0.00023	0.00088	0.00007	0.00023	0.00088
	M	0.00013	0.00041	0.00156	0.00013	0.00041	0.00156	0.00013	0.00041	0.00156
	L	0.00028	0.00089	0.00340	0.00028	0.00089	0.00340	0.00028	0.00089	0.00340
	H	0.00008	0.00025	0.00095	0.00008	0.00025	0.00095	0.00008	0.00025	0.00095
Thaw Settlement	S	0.00004	0.00012	0.00044	0.00004	0.00012	0.00044	0.00004	0.00012	0.00044
	M	0.00006	0.00020	0.00078	0.00006	0.00020	0.00078	0.00006	0.00020	0.00078
	L	0.00014	0.00045	0.00170	0.00014	0.00045	0.00170	0.00014	0.00045	0.00170
	H	0.00004	0.00012	0.00048	0.00004	0.00012	0.00048	0.00004	0.00012	0.00048
Other	S	0.00162	0.01738	0.20869	0.00123	0.01369	0.16613	0.00003	0.00009	0.00033
	M	0.00246	0.03092	0.36929	0.00185	0.02435	0.29399	0.00005	0.00015	0.00059
	L	0.00571	0.06670	0.80303	0.00431	0.05253	0.63928	0.00011	0.00033	0.00128
	H	0.00163	0.01865	0.22480	0.00123	0.01469	0.17896	0.00003	0.00009	0.00036

4.3.2 Arctic Pipeline Fault Tree Frequency Calculations

Incorporation of the frequency effects as variations in and additions to the historical frequencies can be represented in a fault tree, as shown for the large spill size for Arctic pipelines in Figure 4.4. In this figure, the historical frequency as well as that associated with small, medium, and deep-water zones are shown under each of the event boxes. Each box is further split into two, for pipelines less than or at least 10" diameter as represented in the historical database. Such fault trees were developed for all of the pipeline spill sizes, and these additional spill size fault trees, for small, medium, large, and huge spills are presented in Appendix 2, where the complete calculations are given.

Of greatest importance, however, are the pipeline failure frequencies or failure rates per km-yr calculated from the first and second order input distributions using Monte Carlo simulation. These failure rates for the entire range of pipeline spill sizes, small, medium, large, and huge, are given in Tables 4.6, 4.7, 4.8, and 4.9, respectively.

Indeed, a huge array of numbers is shown in these tables. Consider Table 4.8, which is the frequency calculation corresponding to the large spill size fault tree shown in Figure 4.4. Consider the bottom line opposite totals. What the table tells us is that the total spill frequency for pipelines < 10" diameter was 5.172 (per 10^5 km-yr) historically. With the first and second order frequency changes attributable to Arctic effects, this frequency is reduced to 4.374 for shallow water, to 4.003 for medium depth water, and to 2.635 for deep water. A similar trend in the reduction of failure frequencies with increasing water depth for pipelines >= 10" is manifested in the right hand side of the table. Because the frequencies per unit pipeline length and operating year are the key drivers in the balance of the analysis, they have been given in the body of the report (in Tables 4.6 to 4.9) for each of the spill sizes for pipelines. Finally, Table 4.10 summarizes the expected values of the pipeline spill frequencies.

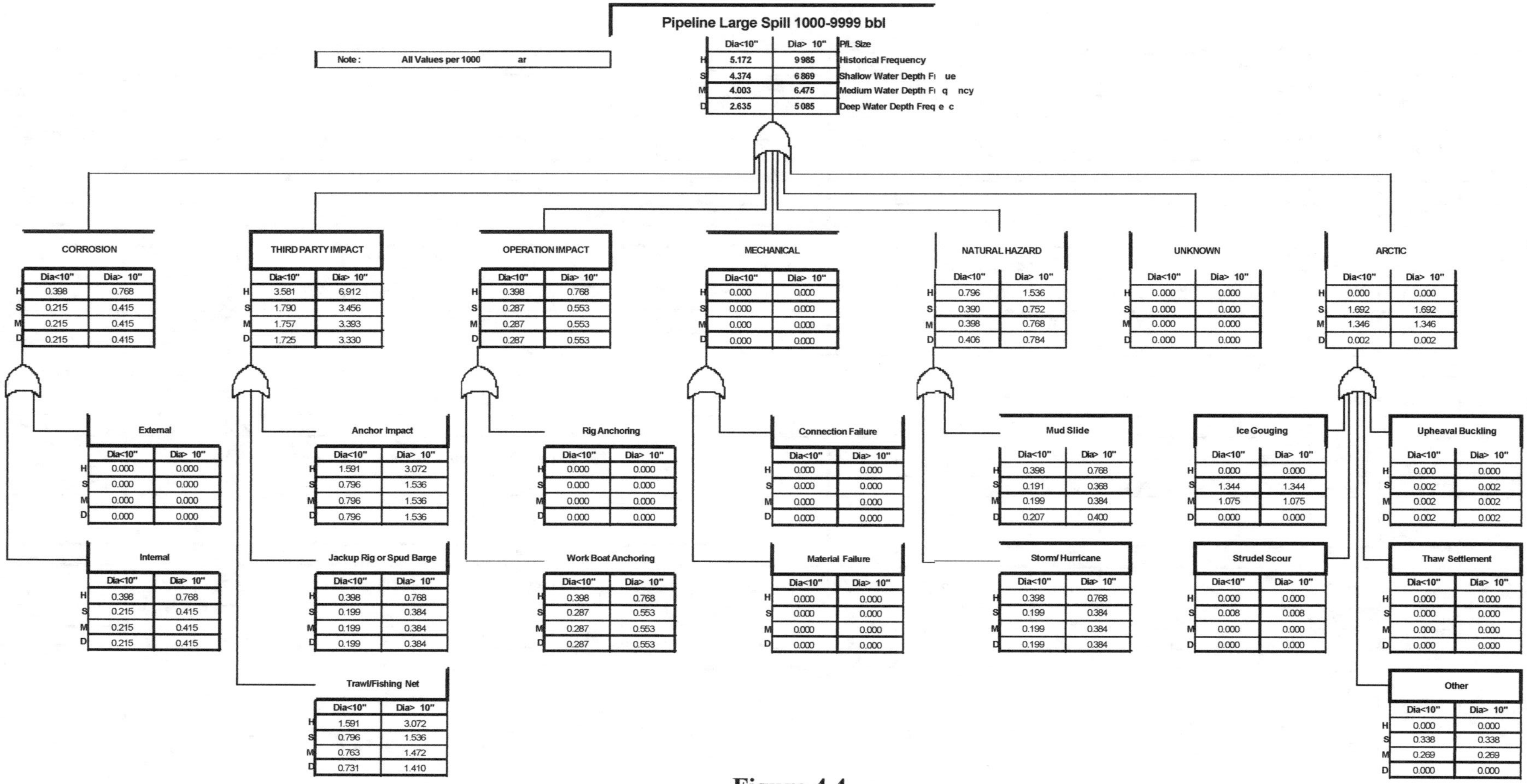

Figure 4.4
Large Spill Frequencies for Pipeline
(Appendix Figure 2.3)

Table 4.6
Arctic Pipeline Small Spill (50-99 bbl) Frequencies
(App. Table 2.3)

CAUSE CLASSIFICATION	HIST. DISTRIBUTION %	Pipeline Diameter <10"										Pipeline Diameter >= 10"									
			Shallow			Medium			Deep				Shallow			Medium			Deep		
		FREQUENCY spills per 10^5km-year	Frequency Change	New Frequency	New Distribution %	Frequency Change	New Frequency	New Distribution %	Frequency Change	New Frequency	New Distribution %	FREQUENCY spills per 10^5km-year	Frequency Change	New Frequency	New Distribution %	Frequency Change	New Frequency	New Distribution %	Frequency Change	New Frequency	New Distribution %
CORROSION	**15.79**	**0.817**	(0.375)	**0.442**	**11.71**	(0.375)	**0.442**	**11.98**	(0.375)	**0.442**	**13.21**	**0.526**	(0.241)	**0.284**	**11.00**	(0.241)	**0.284**	**11.38**	(0.241)	**0.284**	**13.21**
External	5.26	0.272	(0.125)	0.147	3.90	(0.125)	0.147	3.99	(0.125)	0.147	4.40	0.175	(0.080)	0.095	3.67	(0.080)	0.095	3.79	(0.080)	0.095	4.40
Internal	10.53	0.544	(0.250)	0.294	7.81	(0.250)	0.294	7.98	(0.250)	0.294	8.81	0.350	(0.161)	0.190	7.33	(0.161)	0.190	7.59	(0.161)	0.190	8.80
THIRD PARTY IMPACT	**36.84**	**1.905**	(0.953)	**0.953**	**25.25**	(0.958)	**0.947**	**25.68**	(0.964)	**0.942**	**28.15**	**1.226**	(0.613)	**0.613**	**23.72**	(0.617)	**0.609**	**24.40**	(0.620)	**0.606**	**28.15**
Anchor Impact	31.58	1.633	(0.817)	0.817	21.65	(0.817)	0.817	22.14	(0.817)	0.817	24.42	1.051	(0.526)	0.526	20.33	(0.526)	0.526	21.04	(0.526)	0.526	24.41
Jackup Rig or Spud Barge																					
Trawl/Fishing Net	5.26	0.272	(0.136)	0.136	3.61	(0.142)	0.130	3.54	(0.147)	0.125	3.74	0.175	(0.088)	0.088	3.39	(0.091)	0.084	3.36	(0.095)	0.080	3.74
OPERATION IMPACT	**15.79**	**0.817**	(0.228)	**0.588**	**15.60**	(0.228)	**0.588**	**15.95**	(0.228)	**0.588**	**17.59**	**0.526**	(0.147)	**0.379**	**14.65**	(0.147)	**0.379**	**15.16**	(0.147)	**0.379**	**17.59**
Rig Anchoring	5.26	0.272	(0.076)	0.196	5.20	(0.076)	0.196	5.32	(0.076)	0.196	5.86	0.175	(0.049)	0.126	4.88	(0.049)	0.126	5.05	(0.049)	0.126	5.86
Work Boat Anchoring	10.53	0.544	(0.152)	0.392	10.40	(0.152)	0.392	10.63	(0.152)	0.392	11.73	0.350	(0.098)	0.252	9.77	(0.098)	0.252	10.10	(0.098)	0.252	11.73
MECHANICAL	**10.53**	**0.544**		**0.544**	**14.43**		**0.544**	**14.76**		**0.544**	**16.28**	**0.350**		**0.350**	**13.55**		**0.350**	**14.02**		**0.350**	**16.28**
Connection Failure	5.26	0.272		0.272	7.22		0.272	7.38		0.272	8.14	0.175		0.175	6.78		0.175	7.01		0.175	8.14
Material Failure	5.26	0.272		0.272	7.22		0.272	7.38		0.272	8.14	0.175		0.175	6.78		0.175	7.01		0.175	8.14
NATURAL HAZARD	**10.53**	**0.544**	(0.283)	**0.261**	**6.92**	(0.272)	**0.272**	**7.38**	(0.261)	**0.283**	**8.48**	**0.350**	(0.182)	**0.168**	**6.50**	(0.175)	**0.175**	**7.01**	(0.168)	**0.182**	**8.48**
Mud Slide	10.53	0.544	(0.283)	0.261	6.92	(0.272)	0.272	7.38	(0.261)	0.283	8.48	0.350	(0.182)	0.168	6.50	(0.175)	0.175	7.01	(0.168)	0.182	8.48
Storm/ Hurricane																					
ARCTIC			**0.440**	**0.440**	**11.66**	**0.350**	**0.350**	**9.49**	**0.001**	**0.001**	**0.02**		**0.440**	**0.440**	**17.03**	**0.350**	**0.350**	**14.01**	**0.001**	**0.001**	**0.02**
Ice Gouging			0.3495	0.3495	9.26	0.2796	0.2796	7.58					0.3495	0.3495	13.52	0.2796	0.2796	11.19			
Strudel Scour			0.0021	0.0021	0.06								0.0021	0.0021	0.08						
Upheaval Buckling			0.0004	0.0004	0.01	0.0004	0.0004	0.01	0.0004	0.0004	0.01		0.0004	0.0004	0.02	0.0004	0.0004	0.02	0.0004	0.0004	0.02
Thaw Settlement																					
Other			0.0880	0.0880	2.33	0.0700	0.0700	1.90	0.0001	0.0001	0.00		0.0880	0.0880	3.41	0.0700	0.0700	2.80	0.0001	0.0001	0.00
UNKNOWN	**10.53**	**0.544**		**0.544**	**14.43**		**0.544**	**14.76**		**0.544**	**16.28**	**0.350**		**0.350**	**13.55**		**0.350**	**14.02**		**0.350**	**16.28**
TOTALS	**100.00**	**5.172**	(1.399)	**3.773**	**100.00**	(1.484)	**3.688**	**100.00**	(1.827)	**3.345**	**100.00**	**3.328**	(0.744)	**2.585**	**100.00**	(0.830)	**2.498**	**100.00**	(1.176)	**2.152**	**100.00**

Table 4.7
Arctic Pipeline Medium Spill (100-999 bbl) Frequencies
(App. Table 2.4)

CAUSE CLASSIFICATION	HIST. DISTRIBUTION %	Pipeline Diameter <10"										Pipeline Diameter >= 10"									
			Shallow			Medium			Deep				Shallow			Medium			Deep		
		FREQUENCY spills per 10⁵km-year	Frequency Change	New Frequency	New Distribution %	Frequency Change	New Frequency	New Distribution %	Frequency Change	New Frequency	New Distribution %	FREQUENCY spills per 10⁵km-year	Frequency Change	New Frequency	New Distribution %	Frequency Change	New Frequency	New Distribution %	Frequency Change	New Frequency	New Distribution %
CORROSION	**15.79**	**1.429**	(0.656)	**0.773**	**11.70**	(0.656)	**0.773**	**11.97**	(0.656)	**0.773**	**13.21**	**1.577**	(0.724)	**0.853**	**11.83**	(0.724)	**0.853**	**12.07**	(0.724)	**0.853**	**13.21**
External	5.26	0.476	(0.219)	0.258	3.90	(0.219)	0.258	3.99	(0.219)	0.258	4.40	0.526	(0.241)	0.284	3.94	(0.241)	0.284	4.02	(0.241)	0.284	4.40
Internal	10.53	0.953	(0.437)	0.515	7.80	(0.437)	0.515	7.98	(0.437)	0.515	8.81	1.051	(0.482)	0.569	7.88	(0.482)	0.569	8.05	(0.482)	0.569	8.81
THIRD PARTY IMPACT	**36.84**	**3.335**	(1.667)	**1.667**	**25.22**	(1.677)	**1.657**	**25.65**	(1.687)	**1.648**	**28.15**	**3.679**	(1.839)	**1.839**	**25.50**	(1.850)	**1.828**	**25.89**	(1.861)	**1.818**	**28.15**
Anchor Impact	31.58	2.858	(1.429)	1.429	21.62	(1.429)	1.429	22.12	(1.429)	1.429	24.42	3.153	(1.577)	1.577	21.86	(1.577)	1.577	22.32	(1.577)	1.577	24.42
Jackup Rig or Spud Barge																					
Trawl/Fishing Net	5.26	0.476	(0.238)	0.238	3.60	(0.248)	0.228	3.53	(0.258)	0.219	3.74	0.526	(0.263)	0.263	3.64	(0.274)	0.252	3.57	(0.284)	0.241	3.74
OPERATION IMPACT	**15.79**	**1.429**	(0.399)	**1.030**	**15.58**	(0.399)	**1.030**	**15.94**	(0.399)	**1.030**	**17.59**	**1.577**	(0.441)	**1.136**	**15.75**	(0.441)	**1.136**	**16.08**	(0.441)	**1.136**	**17.59**
Rig Anchoring	5.26	0.476	(0.133)	0.343	5.19	(0.133)	0.343	5.31	(0.133)	0.343	5.86	0.526	(0.147)	0.379	5.25	(0.147)	0.379	5.36	(0.147)	0.379	5.86
Work Boat Anchoring	10.53	0.953	(0.266)	0.686	10.38	(0.266)	0.686	10.62	(0.266)	0.686	11.73	1.051	(0.294)	0.757	10.50	(0.294)	0.757	10.72	(0.294)	0.757	11.73
MECHANICAL	**10.53**	**0.953**		**0.953**	**14.41**		**0.953**	**14.75**		**0.953**	**16.28**	**1.051**		**1.051**	**14.57**		**1.051**	**14.88**		**1.051**	**16.28**
Connection Failure	5.26	0.476		0.476	7.21		0.476	7.37		0.476	8.14	0.526		0.526	7.29		0.526	7.44		0.526	8.14
Material Failure	5.26	0.476		0.476	7.21		0.476	7.37		0.476	8.14	0.526		0.526	7.29		0.526	7.44		0.526	8.14
NATURAL HAZARD	**10.53**	**0.953**	(0.496)	**0.457**	**6.91**	(0.476)	**0.476**	**7.37**	(0.457)	**0.496**	**8.48**	**1.051**	(0.547)	**0.504**	**6.98**	(0.526)	**0.526**	**7.44**	(0.504)	**0.547**	**8.48**
Mud Slide	10.53	0.953	(0.496)	0.457	6.91	(0.476)	0.476	7.37	(0.457)	0.496	8.48	1.051	(0.547)	0.504	6.98	(0.526)	0.526	7.44	(0.504)	0.547	8.48
Storm/ Hurricane																					
ARCTIC			**0.778**	**0.778**	**11.77**	**0.619**	**0.619**	**9.58**	**0.001**	**0.001**	**0.02**		**0.778**	**0.778**	**10.79**	**0.619**	**0.619**	**8.76**	**0.001**	**0.001**	**0.01**
Ice Gouging			0.6178	0.6178	9.35	0.4943	0.4943	7.65					0.6178	0.6178	8.57	0.4943	0.4943	7.00			
Strudel Scour			0.0038	0.0038	0.06								0.0038	0.0038	0.05						
Upheaval Buckling			0.0008	0.0008	0.01	0.0008	0.0008	0.01	0.0008	0.0008	0.01		0.0008	0.0008	0.01	0.0008	0.0008	0.01	0.0008	0.0008	0.01
Thaw Settlement																					
Other			0.1556	0.1556	2.35	0.1238	0.1238	1.92	0.0002	0.0002	0.00		0.1556	0.1556	2.16	0.1238	0.1238	1.75	0.0002	0.0002	0.00
UNKNOWN	**10.53**	**0.953**		**0.953**	**14.41**		**0.953**	**14.75**		**0.953**	**16.28**	**1.051**		**1.051**	**14.57**		**1.051**	**14.88**		**1.051**	**16.28**
TOTALS	**100.00**	**9.051**	(2.441)	**6.610**	**100.00**	(2.590)	**6.461**	**100.00**	(3.198)	**5.853**	**100.00**	**9.985**	(2.773)	**7.212**	**100.00**	(2.921)	**7.063**	**100.00**	(3.528)	**6.457**	**100.00**

Table 4.8
Arctic Pipeline Large Spill (1,000-9,999 bbl) Frequencies
(App. Table 2.5)

CAUSE CLASSIFICATION	HIST. DISTRIBUTION %	Pipeline Diameter <10" FREQUENCY spills per 10⁵km-year	Pipeline Diameter <10" Shallow Frequency Change	Pipeline Diameter <10" Shallow New Frequency	Pipeline Diameter <10" Shallow New Distribution %	Pipeline Diameter <10" Medium Frequency Change	Pipeline Diameter <10" Medium New Frequency	Pipeline Diameter <10" Medium New Distribution %	Pipeline Diameter <10" Deep Frequency Change	Pipeline Diameter <10" Deep New Frequency	Pipeline Diameter <10" Deep New Distribution %	Pipeline Diameter >= 10" FREQUENCY spills per 10⁵km-year	Pipeline Diameter >= 10" Shallow Frequency Change	Pipeline Diameter >= 10" Shallow New Frequency	Pipeline Diameter >= 10" Shallow New Distribution %	Pipeline Diameter >= 10" Medium Frequency Change	Pipeline Diameter >= 10" Medium New Frequency	Pipeline Diameter >= 10" Medium New Distribution %	Pipeline Diameter >= 10" Deep Frequency Change	Pipeline Diameter >= 10" Deep New Frequency	Pipeline Diameter >= 10" Deep New Distribution %
CORROSION	**7.69**	**0.398**	(0.183)	**0.215**	**4.92**	(0.183)	**0.215**	**5.38**	(0.183)	**0.215**	**8.17**	**0.768**	(0.353)	**0.415**	**6.05**	(0.353)	**0.415**	**6.42**	(0.353)	**0.415**	**8.17**
External																					
Internal	7.69	0.398	(0.183)	0.215	4.92	(0.183)	0.215	5.38	(0.183)	0.215	8.17	0.768	(0.353)	0.415	6.05	(0.353)	0.415	6.42	(0.353)	0.415	8.17
THIRD PARTY IMPACT	**69.23**	**3.581**	(1.790)	**1.790**	**40.93**	(1.823)	**1.757**	**43.90**	(1.855)	**1.725**	**65.47**	**6.912**	(3.456)	**3.456**	**50.31**	(3.520)	**3.393**	**52.39**	(3.582)	**3.330**	**65.49**
Anchor Impact	30.77	1.591	(0.796)	0.796	18.19	(0.796)	0.796	19.88	(0.796)	0.796	30.20	3.072	(1.536)	1.536	22.36	(1.536)	1.536	23.72	(1.536)	1.536	30.21
Jackup Rig or Spud Barge	7.69	0.398	(0.199)	0.199	4.55	(0.199)	0.199	4.97	(0.199)	0.199	7.55	0.768	(0.384)	0.384	5.59	(0.384)	0.384	5.93	(0.384)	0.384	7.55
Trawl/Fishing Net	30.77	1.591	(0.796)	0.796	18.19	(0.829)	0.763	19.05	(0.861)	0.731	27.72	3.072	(1.536)	1.536	22.36	(1.600)	1.472	22.74	(1.662)	1.410	27.73
OPERATION IMPACT	**7.69**	**0.398**	(0.111)	**0.287**	**6.55**	(0.111)	**0.287**	**7.16**	(0.111)	**0.287**	**10.88**	**0.768**	(0.215)	**0.553**	**8.06**	(0.215)	**0.553**	**8.55**	(0.215)	**0.553**	**10.88**
Rig Anchoring																					
Work Boat Anchoring	7.69	0.398	(0.111)	0.287	6.55	(0.111)	0.287	7.16	(0.111)	0.287	10.88	0.768	(0.215)	0.553	8.06	(0.215)	0.553	8.55	(0.215)	0.553	10.88
MECHANICAL																					
Connection Failure																					
Material Failure																					
NATURAL HAZARD	**15.38**	**0.796**	(0.406)	**0.390**	**8.91**	(0.398)	**0.398**	**9.94**	(0.390)	**0.406**	**15.41**	**1.536**	(0.784)	**0.752**	**10.95**	(0.768)	**0.768**	**11.86**	(0.752)	**0.784**	**15.42**
Mud Slide	7.69	0.398	(0.207)	0.191	4.36	(0.199)	0.199	4.97	(0.191)	0.207	7.86	0.768	(0.400)	0.368	5.36	(0.384)	0.384	5.93	(0.368)	0.400	7.86
Storm/ Hurricane	7.69	0.398	(0.199)	0.199	4.55	(0.199)	0.199	4.97	(0.199)	0.199	7.55	0.768	(0.384)	0.384	5.59	(0.384)	0.384	5.93	(0.384)	0.384	7.55
ARCTIC			**1.692**	**1.692**	**38.69**	**1.346**	**1.346**	**33.62**	**0.002**	**0.002**	**0.08**		**1.692**	**1.692**	**24.63**	**1.346**	**1.346**	**20.78**	**0.002**	**0.002**	**0.04**
Ice Gouging			1.3438	1.3438	30.72	1.0750	1.0750	26.86					1.3438	1.3438	19.56	1.0750	1.0750	16.60			
Strudel Scour			0.0082	0.0082	0.19								0.0082	0.0082	0.12						
Upheaval Buckling			0.0016	0.0016	0.04	0.0016	0.0016	0.04	0.0016	0.0016	0.06		0.0016	0.0016	0.02	0.0016	0.0016	0.03	0.0016	0.0016	0.03
Thaw Settlement																					
Other			0.3384	0.3384	7.74	0.2692	0.2692	6.72	0.0004	0.0004	0.02		0.3384	0.3384	4.93	0.2692	0.2692	4.16	0.0004	0.0004	0.01
UNKNOWN																					
TOTALS	**100.00**	**5.172**	(0.798)	**4.374**	**100.00**	(1.169)	**4.003**	**100.00**	(2.537)	**2.635**	**100.00**	**9.985**	(3.115)	**6.869**	**100.00**	(3.509)	**6.475**	**100.00**	(4.899)	**5.085**	**100.00**

Table 4.9
Arctic Pipeline Huge Spill (>= 10,000 bbl) Frequencies
(App. Table 2.6)

CAUSE CLASSIFICATION	HIST. DISTRIBUTION %	*Pipeline Diameter <10"* FREQUENCY spills per 10^5km-year	Shallow			Medium			Deep			*Pipeline Diameter >= 10"* FREQUENCY spills per 10^5km-year	Shallow			Medium			Deep		
			Frequency Change	New Frequency	New Distribution %	Frequency Change	New Frequency	New Distribution %	Frequency Change	New Frequency	New Distribution %		Frequency Change	New Frequency	New Distribution %	Frequency Change	New Frequency	New Distribution %	Frequency Change	New Frequency	New Distribution %
CORROSION	**7.69**	**0.099**	(0.046)	**0.054**	**4.70**	(0.046)	**0.054**	**5.17**	(0.046)	**0.054**	**8.17**	**0.256**	(0.118)	**0.138**	**6.30**	(0.118)	**0.138**	**6.64**	(0.118)	**0.138**	**8.17**
External																					
Internal	7.69	0.099	(0.046)	0.054	4.70	(0.046)	0.054	5.17	(0.046)	0.054	8.17	0.256	(0.118)	0.138	6.30	(0.118)	0.138	6.64	(0.118)	0.138	8.17
THIRD PARTY IMPACT	**69.23**	**0.895**	(0.448)	**0.448**	**39.12**	(0.456)	**0.439**	**42.20**	(0.464)	**0.431**	**65.46**	**2.304**	(1.152)	**1.152**	**52.38**	(1.173)	**1.131**	**54.20**	(1.194)	**1.110**	**65.50**
Anchor Impact	30.77	0.398	(0.199)	0.199	17.39	(0.199)	0.199	19.11	(0.199)	0.199	30.19	1.024	(0.512)	0.512	23.28	(0.512)	0.512	24.54	(0.512)	0.512	30.21
Jackup Rig or Spud Barge	7.69	0.099	(0.050)	0.050	4.35	(0.050)	0.050	4.78	(0.050)	0.050	7.55	0.256	(0.128)	0.128	5.82	(0.128)	0.128	6.13	(0.128)	0.128	7.55
Trawl/Fishing Net	30.77	0.398	(0.199)	0.199	17.39	(0.207)	0.191	18.32	(0.215)	0.183	27.72	1.024	(0.512)	0.512	23.28	(0.533)	0.491	23.52	(0.554)	0.470	27.74
OPERATION IMPACT	**7.69**	**0.099**	(0.028)	**0.072**	**6.26**	(0.028)	**0.072**	**6.88**	(0.028)	**0.072**	**10.88**	**0.256**	(0.072)	**0.184**	**8.39**	(0.072)	**0.184**	**8.84**	(0.072)	**0.184**	**10.88**
Rig Anchoring																					
Work Boat Anchoring	7.69	0.099	(0.028)	0.072	6.26	(0.028)	0.072	6.88	(0.028)	0.072	10.88	0.256	(0.072)	0.184	8.39	(0.072)	0.184	8.84	(0.072)	0.184	10.88
MECHANICAL																					
Connection Failure																					
Material Failure																					
NATURAL HAZARD	**15.38**	**0.199**	(0.102)	**0.097**	**8.51**	(0.099)	**0.099**	**9.55**	(0.097)	**0.102**	**15.41**	**0.512**	(0.261)	**0.251**	**11.40**	(0.256)	**0.256**	**12.27**	(0.251)	**0.261**	**15.42**
Mud Slide	7.69	0.099	(0.052)	0.048	4.17	(0.050)	0.050	4.78	(0.048)	0.052	7.86	0.256	(0.133)	0.123	5.58	(0.128)	0.128	6.13	(0.123)	0.133	7.87
Storm/ Hurricane	7.69	0.099	(0.050)	0.050	4.35	(0.050)	0.050	4.78	(0.050)	0.050	7.55	0.256	(0.128)	0.128	5.82	(0.128)	0.128	6.13	(0.128)	0.128	7.55
ARCTIC			**0.474**	**0.474**	**41.40**	**0.377**	**0.377**	**36.19**	**0.001**	**0.001**	**0.09**		**0.474**	**0.474**	**21.54**	**0.377**	**0.377**	**18.06**	**0.001**	**0.001**	**0.03**
Ice Gouging			0.3762	0.3762	32.88	0.3010	0.3010	28.91					0.3762	0.3762	17.11	0.3010	0.3010	14.42			
Strudel Scour			0.0023	0.0023	0.20								0.0023	0.0023	0.10						
Upheaval Buckling			0.0005	0.0005	0.04	0.0005	0.0005	0.04	0.0005	0.0005	0.07		0.0005	0.0005	0.02	0.0005	0.0005	0.02	0.0005	0.0005	0.03
Thaw Settlement																					
Other			0.0947	0.0947	8.28	0.0754	0.0754	7.24	0.0001	0.0001	0.02		0.0947	0.0947	4.31	0.0754	0.0754	3.61	0.0001	0.0001	0.01
UNKNOWN																					
TOTALS	**100.00**	**1.293**	(0.149)	**1.144**	**100.00**	(0.252)	**1.041**	**100.00**	(0.634)	**0.659**	**100.00**	**3.328**	(1.129)	**2.199**	**100.00**	(1.242)	**2.087**	**100.00**	(1.633)	**1.695**	**100.00**

Table 4.10
Arctic Pipeline Spill Frequencies Expected Value Summary
(App. Table 2.2A)

Pipeline Spill Size	PipelineDiameter <10"				Pipeline Diameter >=10"			
	Historical Frequency spills per 10^5km-year	Arctic Frequency			Historical Frequency spills per 10^5km-year	Arctic Frequency		
		Shallow	Medium	Deep		Shallow	Medium	Deep
SMALL SPILLS 50-99 bbl	5.172	3.671	3.587	3.243	3.328	2.519	2.433	2.087
MEDIUM SPILLS 100-999 bbl	9.051	6.432	6.283	5.676	8.320	5.975	5.826	5.218
LARGE SPILLS 1000-9999 bbl	5.172	4.374	4.003	2.635	9.985	6.870	6.476	5.086
HUGE SPILLS >=10000 bbl	1.293	1.144	1.041	0.659	3.328	2.200	2.087	1.695

4.4 Platform Fault Tree Analysis

4.4.1 Arctic Platform Spill Causal Frequency Distributions

Table 4.11 summarizes the variations in the modified and unique Arctic effect inputs for platforms. As for pipeline unique effects, both the Triangular Distribution expected and modal values are given.

The first three modified cause classifications, the process facility release, storage tank release, and structural failure were reduced by 20 to 30% primarily as a result of the state-of-the-art engineering, construction, and operational standards and practices expected. As before, storms tend to be less severe in the Arctic, and certainly during the ice season would have limited impact on the facility. Due to the extremely low traffic density, as for the case of pipelines, the ship collision cause has been reduced by 50%.

Unique effects are also included. Increments in facility spills were attributed to ice force, low temperature effects, and unknown effects which were taken as a percentage of the other unique Arctic effects. Ice force effect calculations were based on the 1/10,000 year ice force causing spills, predominantly small and medium. Ice forces are also considered to increase as a contributor to oil spill occurrences with water depth, due to the increasing severity of ice loads as one moves towards the edge of the landfast ice zone with increasing water depth. Increase of low temperature effects with water depth was estimated as 10% of historical process facility spill rates.

Changes in frequency distribution attributable to Arctic effects were calculated using the secondary effect probability distribution, as was done for pipelines. Table 4.12 summarizes the principal distribution parameters for both the Arctic modified and Arctic unique effect distributions.

4.4.2 Arctic Platform Fault Tree Spill Frequency Calculations

Figure 4.5 shows the fault tree developed for Arctic platform spills for the different water depth zones for large and huge spill sizes, which were grouped together as described for platforms in Chapter 2. Again, the fault tree gives the historical value, together with the calculated values for shallow, medium, and deep water. In the case of this particular fault tree, there was room to represent both the small and medium or less than 1,000 bbl and the large and huge or at least 1,000 bbl spills. Like pipelines, it is evident that platforms manifest a somewhat lower frequency for both spill size categories for the Arctic conditions. Tables 4.13 and 4.14 show the frequency calculations for platforms for small and medium and large and huge spill sizes, respectively. Table 4.15 summarizes the historical and derived Arctic expected values of platform spill frequencies.

Table 4.11
Platform Arctic Effect Derivation Summary
(App. Table 2.7)

CAUSE CLASSIFICATION	Spill Size	Historical Expected Frequency Change %			Reason
		Shallow	Medium	Deep	
PROCESS FACILITY RLS.	All	(30)	(30)	(30)	State of the art now, High QC, High Inspection and Maintenance Requirements
STORAGE TANK RLS.	All	(30)	(30)	(30)	State of the art now, High QC, High Inspection and Maintenance Requirements
STRUCTURAL FAILURE	All	(20)	(20)	(20)	High safety factor, Monitoring Programs
HURRICANE/STORM	All	(50)	(40)	(30)	Less severe storms. More intensity in deep water.
COLLISION	All	(50)	(50)	(50)	Very low traffic density.
		Freq. Increment per 10^4 well-year			
		Expected	Expected	Expected	
		Mode	Mode	Mode	
ARCTIC					
Ice Force	SM	0.1447	0.2170	0.3256	Assumed 10,000 year return period ice force causes spill 4% of occurrences (96% reliability). 85% of the spills are SM.
		0.0340	0.0510	0.0765	
	LH	0.0255	0.0383	0.0575	
		0.0060	0.0090	0.0135	
Facility Low Temperature	SM	0.1000	0.1000	0.1000	Assumed fraction of Historical Process Facilities release frequency with 6% SM and 3% for LH spill sizes.
		0.1000	0.1000	0.1000	
	LH	0.0080	0.0080	0.0080	
		0.0080	0.0080	0.0080	
Other	SM	0.0244	0.0316	0.0424	10% of sum of above.
		0.0134	0.0151	0.0177	
	LH	0.0033	0.0046	0.0065	
		0.0014	0.0017	0.0022	

Table 4.12
Platform Arctic Effect Distribution Derivation Summary
(App. Table 2.8)

CAUSE CLASSIFICATION	Spill Size	Shallow			Medium			Deep		
		Frequency Change %								
		Min	Mode	Max	Min	Mode	Max	Min	Mode	Max
PROCESS FACILITY RLS.	All	(60)	(30)	(10)	(60)	(30)	(10)	(60)	(30)	(10)
STORAGE TANK RLS.	All	(60)	(30)	(10)	(60)	(30)	(10)	(60)	(30)	(10)
STRUCTURAL FAILURE	All	(60)	(20)	(10)	(60)	(20)	(10)	(60)	(20)	(10)
HURRICANE/STORM	All	(90)	(50)	(10)	(90)	(40)	(10)	(90)	(30)	(10)
COLLISION	All	(90)	(50)	(10)	(90)	(50)	(10)	(90)	(50)	(10)
		Frequency Increment per 10^4 well-year								
ARCTIC										
Ice Force	SM	0.003	0.034	0.340	0.005	0.051	0.510	0.008	0.077	0.765
	LH	0.001	0.006	0.060	0.001	0.009	0.090	0.001	0.014	0.135
Facility Low Temperature	SM	0.050	0.100	0.150	0.050	0.100	0.150	0.050	0.100	0.150
	LH	0.004	0.008	0.012	0.004	0.008	0.012	0.004	0.008	0.012
Other	SM	0.005	0.013	0.049	0.006	0.015	0.066	0.006	0.018	0.092
	LH	0.000	0.001	0.007	0.000	0.002	0.010	0.001	0.002	0.015

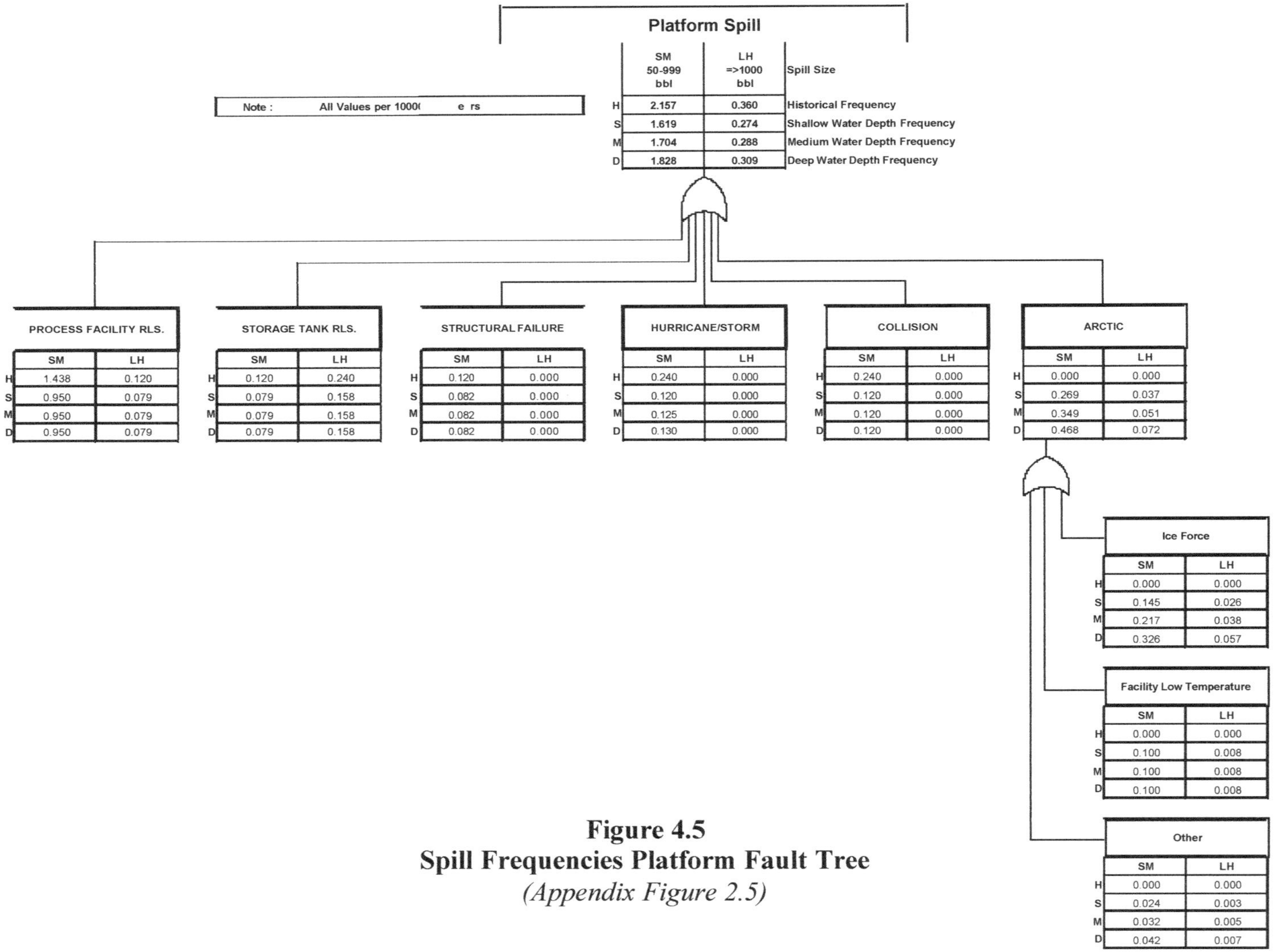
Platform Spill
SM 50-999 bbl | LH =>1000 bbl | Spill Size
H 2.157 0.360 Historical Frequency
S 1.619 0.274 Shallow Water Depth Frequency
M 1.704 0.288 Medium Water Depth Frequency
D 1.828 0.309 Deep Water Depth Frequency
Note : All Values per 1000(e rs
PROCESS FACILITY RLS.
SM LH
H 1.438 0.120
S 0.950 0.079
M 0.950 0.079
D 0.950 0.079
STORAGE TANK RLS.
SM LH
H 0.120 0.240
S 0.079 0.158
M 0.079 0.158
D 0.079 0.158
STRUCTURAL FAILURE
SM LH
H 0.120 0.000
S 0.082 0.000
M 0.082 0.000
D 0.082 0.000
HURRICANE/STORM
SM LH
H 0.240 0.000
S 0.120 0.000
M 0.125 0.000
D 0.130 0.000
COLLISION
SM LH
H 0.240 0.000
S 0.120 0.000
M 0.120 0.000
D 0.120 0.000
ARCTIC
SM LH
H 0.000 0.000
S 0.269 0.037
M 0.349 0.051
D 0.468 0.072
Ice Force
SM LH
H 0.000 0.000
S 0.145 0.026
M 0.217 0.038
D 0.326 0.057
Facility Low Temperature
SM LH
H 0.000 0.000
S 0.100 0.008
M 0.100 0.008
D 0.100 0.008
Other
SM LH
H 0.000 0.000
S 0.024 0.003
M 0.032 0.005
D 0.042 0.007

Figure 4.5
Spill Frequencies Platform Fault Tree
(Appendix Figure 2.5)

Table 4.13
Arctic Platform Small and Medium Spill Frequencies
(App. Table 2.9)

CAUSE CLASSIFICATION	HISTORICAL DISTRIBUTION %	SMALL AND MEDIUM SPILLS 50-999 bbl									
		FREQUENCY spills per 10^4 well-year	Shallow			Medium			Deep		
			Frequency Change	New Frequency	New Distribution %	Frequency Change	New Frequency	New Distribution %	Frequency Change	New Frequency	New Distribution %
PROCESS FACILITY RLS.	66.67	1.438	(0.488)	0.950	58.65	(0.488)	0.950	55.74	(0.488)	0.950	51.96
STORAGE TANK RLS.	5.56	0.120	(0.041)	0.079	4.89	(0.041)	0.079	4.65	(0.041)	0.079	4.33
STRUCTURAL FAILURE	5.56	0.120	(0.038)	0.082	5.04	(0.038)	0.082	4.79	(0.038)	0.082	4.46
HURRICANE/STORM	11.11	0.240	(0.120)	0.120	7.40	(0.115)	0.125	7.33	(0.110)	0.130	7.09
COLLISION	11.11	0.240	(0.120)	0.120	7.40	(0.120)	0.120	7.03	(0.120)	0.120	6.56
ARCTIC			0.269	0.269	16.62	0.349	0.349	20.46	0.468	0.468	25.60
Ice Force			0.145	0.145	8.94	0.217	0.217	12.74	0.326	0.326	17.81
Facility Low Temperature			0.100	0.100	6.18	0.100	0.100	5.87	0.100	0.100	5.47
Other			0.024	0.024	1.51	0.032	0.032	1.86	0.042	0.042	2.32
TOTALS	100.00	2.157	(0.538)	1.619	100.00	(0.453)	1.704	100.00	(0.329)	1.828	100.00

Table 4.14
Arctic Platform Large and Huge Spill Frequencies
(App. Table 2.10)

CAUSE CLASSIFICATION	HISTORICAL DISTRIBUTION %	LARGE AND HUGE SPILLS >=1000 bbl									
			Shallow			Medium			Deep		
		FREQUENCY spills per 10^4 well-year	Frequency Change	New Frequency	New Distribution %	Frequency Change	New Frequency	New Distribution %	Frequency Change	New Frequency	New Distribution %
PROCESS FACILITY RLS.	33.33	0.120	(0.041)	0.079	28.85	(0.041)	0.079	27.45	(0.041)	0.079	25.58
STORAGE TANK RLS.	66.67	0.240	(0.081)	0.158	57.70	(0.081)	0.158	54.89	(0.081)	0.158	51.16
STRUCTURAL FAILURE											
HURRICANE/STORM											
COLLISION											
ARCTIC			0.037	0.037	13.44	0.051	0.051	17.66	0.072	0.072	23.27
Ice Force			0.026	0.026	9.31	0.038	0.038	13.28	0.057	0.057	18.57
Facility Low Temperature			0.008	0.008	2.92	0.008	0.008	2.77	0.008	0.008	2.59
Other			0.003	0.003	1.22	0.005	0.005	1.60	0.007	0.007	2.11
TOTALS	100.00	0.360	(0.085)	0.274	100.00	(0.071)	0.288	100.00	(0.050)	0.309	100.00

Table 4.15
Arctic Platforms Spill Frequency Expected Value Summary
(App. Table 2.8A)

Platform Spill Size	Historical Frequency spills per 10^4 well-year	Arctic Frequency		
		Shallow	Medium	Deep
SMALL AND MEDIUM SPILLS 50-999 bbl	2.157	1.619	1.704	1.828
LARGE AND HUGE SPILLS >=1,000 bbl	0.360	0.274	0.288	0.309

4.5 Blowout Frequency Analysis

4.5.1 Well Blowout First Order Arctic Effects

The historical data, as described in Chapter 2, was modified for each well type, spill size, and water depth range, as described in Table 4.16. No Arctic unique effects were introduced for well blowouts.

4.5.2 Arctic Well Blowout Spill Frequency Calculation

Table 4.17 gives the details of the frequency calculation for well blowouts. No fault tree was required here, as only base events with no causal distributions were modeled for each case. The modifications given in Table 4.16 were applied to all three values (minimum, mode, maximum) to yield the values summarized in Table 4.17.

4.6 Spill Volume Distributions

Table 4.18 summarizes the spill volume distribution parameters for each facility type, including the expected value that was calculated utilizing a Monte Carlo calculation. The spill volume parameters were derived from the historical data as described in Section 2.7.

Table 4.16
Well Fault Tree Analysis Arctic Effect Summary
(App. Table 2.11)

EVENT	FREQUENCY UNIT	Historical Expected Frequency Change %			Reason
		Shallow	Medium	Deep	
		Small and Medium Spills 50-999 bbl			
PRODUCTION WELL	spill per 10^4 well-year	(30)	(30)	(30)	State of the art now, High QC, High Inspection and Maintenance Requirements
EXPLORATION WELL DRILLING	spill per 10^4 wells	(30)	(20)	(10)	Highly qualified drilling contractor. Better logistics support in shallow water.
DEVELOPMENT WELL DRILLING	spill per 10^4 wells	(30)	(20)	(10)	Highly qualified drilling contractor. Better logistics support in shallow water.
		Large Spills 1000-9999 bbl			
PRODUCTION WELL	spill per 10^4 well-year	(30)	(30)	(30)	State of the art now, High QC, High Inspection and Maintenance Requirements
EXPLORATION WELL DRILLING	spill per 10^4 wells	(30)	(20)	(10)	Highly qualified drilling contractor. Better logistics support in shallow water.
DEVELOPMENT WELL DRILLING	spill per 10^4 wells	(30)	(20)	(10)	Highly qualified drilling contractor. Better logistics support in shallow water.
		Spill 10000-149999 bbl			
PRODUCTION WELL	spill per 10^4 well-year	(30)	(30)	(30)	State of the art now, High QC, High Inspection and Maintenance Requirements
EXPLORATION WELL DRILLING	spill per 10^4 wells	(30)	(20)	(10)	Highly qualified drilling contractor. Better logistics support in shallow water.
DEVELOPMENT WELL DRILLING	spill per 10^4 wells	(30)	(20)	(10)	Highly qualified drilling contractor. Better logistics support in shallow water.
		Spill >=150000 bbl			
PRODUCTION WELL	spill per 10^4 well-year	(30)	(30)	(30)	State of the art now, High QC, High Inspection and Maintenance Requirements
EXPLORATION WELL DRILLING	spill per 10^4 wells	(30)	(20)	(10)	Highly qualified drilling contractor. Better logistics support in shallow water.
DEVELOPMENT WELL DRILLING	spill per 10^4 wells	(30)	(20)	(10)	Highly qualified drilling contractor. Better logistics support in shallow water.

Table 4.17
Arctic Well Blowout Frequencies
(App. Table 2.12)

EVENT	FREQUENCY UNIT	HISTORICAL FREQUENCY	Shallow		Medium		Deep	
			Frequency Change	New Frequency	Frequency Change	New Frequency	Frequency Change	New Frequency
		Small and Medium Spills 50-999 bbl						
PRODUCTION WELL	spill per 10^4 well-year	0.147	-0.044	0.103	-0.044	0.103	-0.044	0.103
EXPLORATION WELL DRILLING	spill per 10^4 wells	2.262	-0.678	1.583	-0.452	1.809	-0.226	2.035
DEVELOPMENT WELL DRILLING	spill per 10^4 wells	0.692	-0.208	0.484	-0.138	0.554	-0.069	0.623
		Large Spills 1000-9999 bbl						
PRODUCTION WELL	spill per 10^4 well-year	1.026	-0.308	0.718	-0.308	0.718	-0.308	0.718
EXPLORATION WELL DRILLING	spill per 10^4 wells	15.824	-4.747	11.077	-3.165	12.659	-1.582	14.242
DEVELOPMENT WELL DRILLING	spill per 10^4 wells	4.833	-1.450	3.383	-0.967	3.867	-0.483	4.350
		Spills 10000-149999 bbl						
PRODUCTION WELL	spill per 10^4 well-year	0.440	-0.132	0.308	-0.132	0.308	-0.132	0.308
EXPLORATION WELL DRILLING	spill per 10^4 wells	6.799	-2.040	4.759	-1.360	5.439	-0.680	6.119
DEVELOPMENT WELL DRILLING	spill per 10^4 wells	2.076	-0.623	1.453	-0.415	1.661	-0.208	1.868
		Spills >=150000 bbl						
PRODUCTION WELL	spill per 10^4 well-year	0.293	-0.088	0.205	-0.088	0.205	-0.088	0.205
EXPLORATION WELL DRILLING	spill per 10^4 wells	3.936	-1.181	2.755	-0.787	3.149	-0.394	3.543
DEVELOPMENT WELL DRILLING	spill per 10^4 wells	2.076	-0.623	1.453	-0.415	1.661	-0.208	1.868

Table 4.18
Summary of Spill Size Distribution Parameters
(App. Table 2.13)

	PIPELINE SPILL VOLUMES															
Spill Size	Small Spills 50-99 bbl				Medium Spills 100-999 bbl				Large Spills 1000-9999 bbl				Huge Spills >=10000 bbl			
Spill Expectation	Low	Mode	High	Expected	Low	Mode	High	Expected	Low	Mode	High	Expected	Low	Mode	High	Expected
Pipelines Diameter 10" Spill	50	58	99	71	100	226	999	485	1000	4436	9999	5279	10000	14423	20000	14880
Pipelines Diameter 10" Spill	50	58	99	71	100	387	999	516	1000	3932	9999	5176	10000	17705	20000	15552

	PLATFORM SPILL VOLUMES							
Spill Size	Small and Medium Spills 50-999 bbl				Large and Huge Spills >=1000 bbl			
Spill Expectation	Low	Mode	High	Expected	Low	Mode	High	Expected
Platform Spill	50	158	999	452	1000	6130	10000	5631

	WELL SPILL VOLUMES															
Spill Size	Small and Medium Spills 50-999 bbl				Large Spills 1000-9999 bbl				Spills 10000-149999 bbl				Spills >=150000 bbl			
Spill Expectation	Low	Mode	High	Expected	Low	Mode	High	Expected	Low	Mode	High	Expected	Low	Mode	High	Expected
Well Spill	50	500	999	519	1000	4500	9999	5292	10000	20000	149999	68349	150000	200000	250000	200000

CHAPTER 5

OIL SPILL OCCURRENCE INDICATOR QUANTIFICATION

5.1 Definition of Oil Spill Occurrence Indicators

Four primary oil spill occurrence indicators (generally referred to as "spill indicators" after this) were quantified in this study. These are as follows:

- Frequency in spills per year.
- Frequency in spills per barrel produced in each year.
- Spill index, the product of spill frequency and associated average spill size.
- Life of field indicators.

The spill indicators defined above are subdivided as follows for this study:

- By scenario (two scenarios).
- By water depth (three ranges).
- By facility type (six types).
- By spill size (four sizes).
- By year (2009 to 2044 is 36 years inclusive).

The above combinations translate into 144 sets of spill indicators per year. Given that these are calculated for each year, with the scenario lasting for 36 years, gives 5,184 sets of indicators. In this chapter, we will try to summarize only the salient results of the indicators; the Appendix 4 gives the full calculation printouts for the Monte Carlo results used in the body of this report.

5.2 Oil Spill Occurrence Indicator Calculation Process

The oil spill occurrence indicator calculation process is shown in the flow chart originally given in Figure 1.2, and again presented as Figure 5.1. This chapter discusses the spill occurrence indicator calculations as shown in the shaded rectangle in Figure 5.1. Previous chapters covered the balance of the items in that figure.

Essentially, this chapter addresses the combining of the development scenarios described in Chapter 3 with the unit-spill frequency distributions presented in Chapter 4 to provide measures of oil spill occurrence, the oil spill indicators. Although the calculation is complex because of the many combinations considered (approximately 5,000), in principle, it is a simple process of accounting. Essentially, the quantities of potential oil spill sources are multiplied by their appropriate unit oil spill frequency to give the total expected spill distributions. To develop the probability distributions by the Monte Carlo process, each of the 5,000 combinations needs to be sampled, in this case a sampling of 5,000 iterations was carried out for each combination studied. This translates into roughly 25 million arithmetic operations to generate the Monte Carlo results.

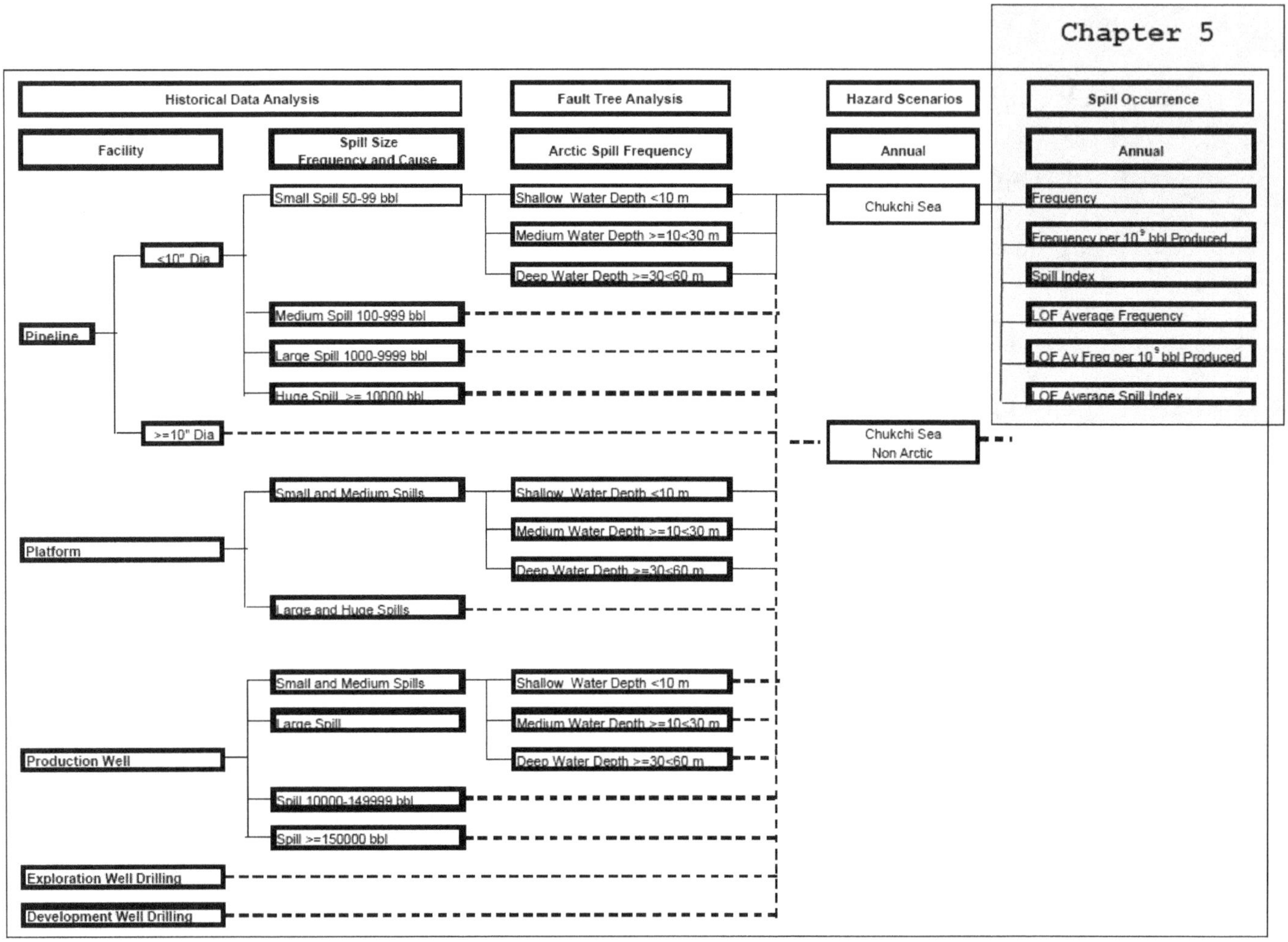
Chapter 5
Historical Data Analysis
Fault Tree Analysis
Hazard Scenarios
Spill Occurrence
Facility
Spill Size Frequency and Cause
Arctic Spill Frequency
Annual
Annual
Small Spill 50-99 bbl
Shallow Water Depth <10 m
Chukchi Sea
Frequency
Medium Water Depth >=10<30 m
Frequency per 10⁹ bbl Produced
<10" Dia
Deep Water Depth >=30<60 m
Spill Index
Medium Spill 100-999 bbl
LOF Average Frequency
Pipeline
Large Spill 1000-9999 bbl
LOF Av Freq per 10⁹ bbl Produced
Huge Spill >= 10000 bbl
LOF Average Spill Index
>=10" Dia
Chukchi Sea Non Arctic
Small and Medium Spills
Shallow Water Depth <10 m
Medium Water Depth >=10<30 m
Platform
Deep Water Depth >=30<60 m
Large and Huge Spills
Small and Medium Spills
Shallow Water Depth <10 m
Large Spill
Medium Water Depth >=10<30 m
Production Well
Deep Water Depth >=30<60 m
Spill 10000-149999 bbl
Spill >=150000 bbl
Exploration Well Drilling
Development Well Drilling

Figure 5.1
Calculation Flow Chart

5.3 Summary of Chukchi Sea Oil Spill Occurrence Indicators

5.3.1 Chukchi Sea Oil Spill Occurrence Indicators

Each of the principal oil spill occurrence indicators calculated for the pipelines, platforms, and wells under Sale 1 for each year is given in Figures 5.2, 5.3, and 5.4.

As can be seen, each of these figures spans the development scenario to year 2044 as described in Table 3.3. Further, each of the indicators has been subdivided into three segments for each year, those corresponding to spills 50-999 bbl (small and medium), spills 1,000-9,999 bbl (large), and spills >=10,000 bbl (huge). It should be noted that the spill frequency associated with each spill size is only the shaded increment shown in each of the bars. Thus, for example, for the year 2030, small and medium spills are approximately 30.0 per thousand years. Next, in that year, large spills are approximately 13.0 per thousand years, as shown in the second bar increment (i.e., 43.0 – 30.0 = 13.0). Finally, the top increment corresponds to huge spills, and is approximately 9.0 per thousand years. The same form of presentation applies for spills per barrel produced and for the spill index shown in Figures 5.3 and 5.4. For years in which no production exists, the spills per barrel produced are not applicable. Clearly, the spill index is dominated by the huge spills. The spills per barrel produced continue to rise to the final production year (2043), because the facility quantities (and hence spill rate) remain relatively high, while production volumes decrease significantly each year. The reader should note that following this detailed presentation of the spill indicators in separate figures, all three spill indicators will be given in one figure in order to conserve space and make the report a little more concise.

Spill indicators by facility type were also quantified. All three spill indicators for pipelines are shown in Figure 5.5. Figure 5.6 shows the spill indicators for platforms and Figure 5.7 shows the spill indicators for drilling of wells and producing wells. The graph ordinate axes have intentionally been kept the same to facilitate comparison. Numerous conclusions can be drawn from the comparison of these spill indicators. For example, it can be seen that the major contributors to spill frequency are platforms. The largest of the facility spill expectations, as represented by spill index, are the wells, simply because they have the potential to release the largest amounts of oil in blowouts.

Finally, as part of the assessment of the Chukchi Sea development scenario, a Monte Carlo analysis was carried out for each year, with the distributed inputs described earlier. The tabular results of the Monte Carlo simulation of 5,000 iterations, is summarized in Table 5.1. This table gives the statistical characteristics of the calculated indicators for each of three spill size ranges, as well as a tabular summary of their cumulative distribution curves for a representative production year (2024). Figure 5.8 shows graphs of the calculated cumulative distribution functions. Basically, the vertical axis gives the probability in percent that the corresponding value on the horizontal axis will not be exceeded. Thus, for example, referring to the central graph, for significant spills >= 1,000 bbl (large and huge), there is a 50% probability that a spill frequency will be no more than 0.25 per billion barrels produced in year 2024.

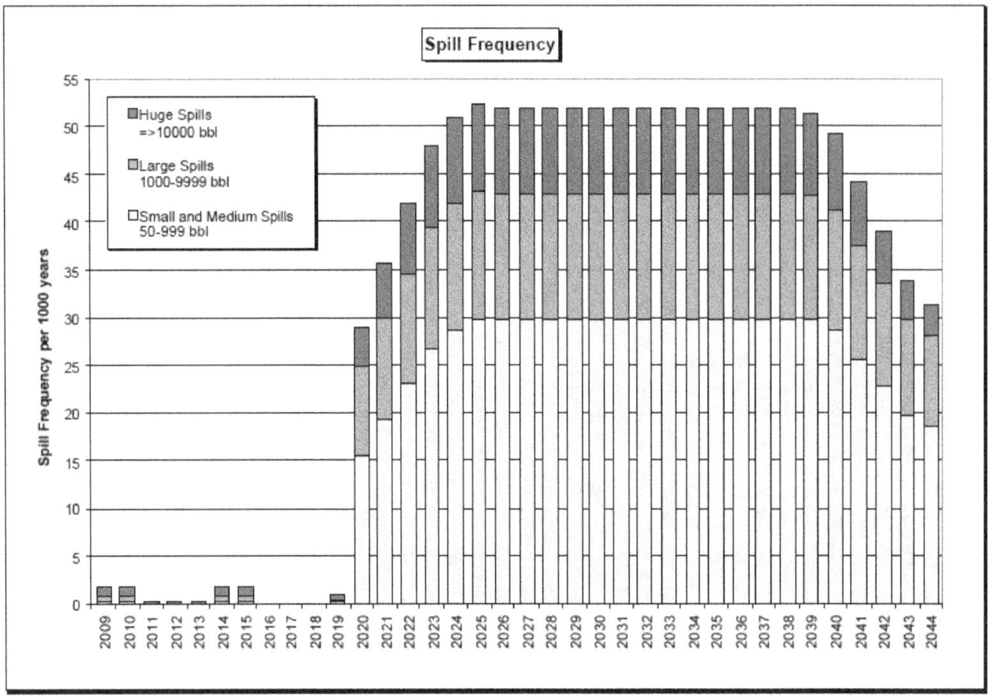

Figure 5.2
Chukchi Sea Spill Frequency per 1,000 Years
(Appendix Figure 4.1.01)

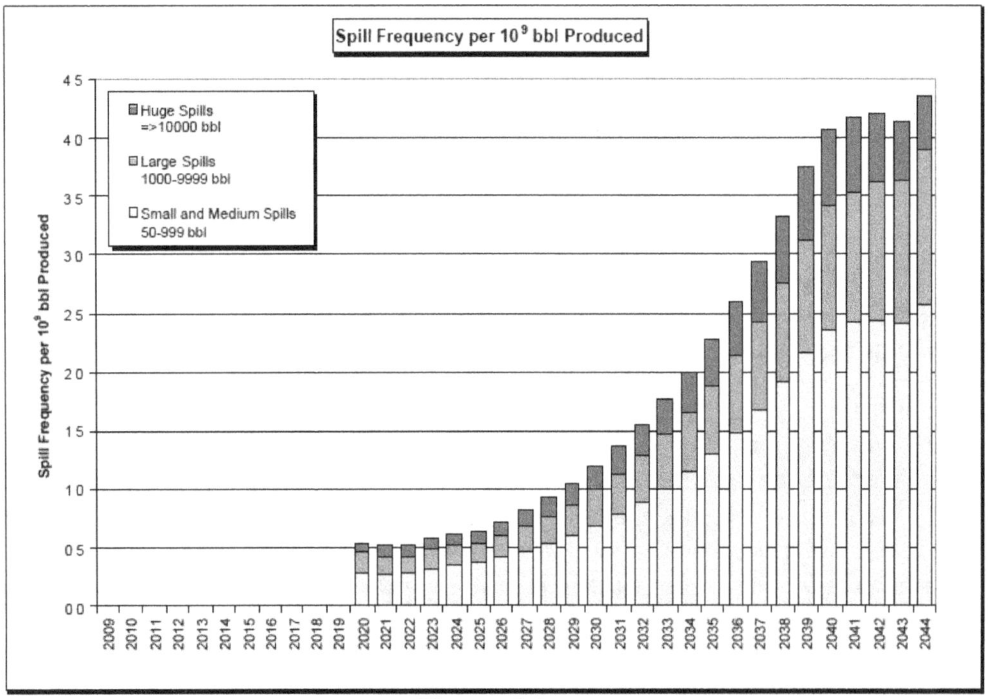

Figure 5.3
Chukchi Sea Spill Frequency per 10^9 Barrels Produced
(Appendix Figure 4.1.02)

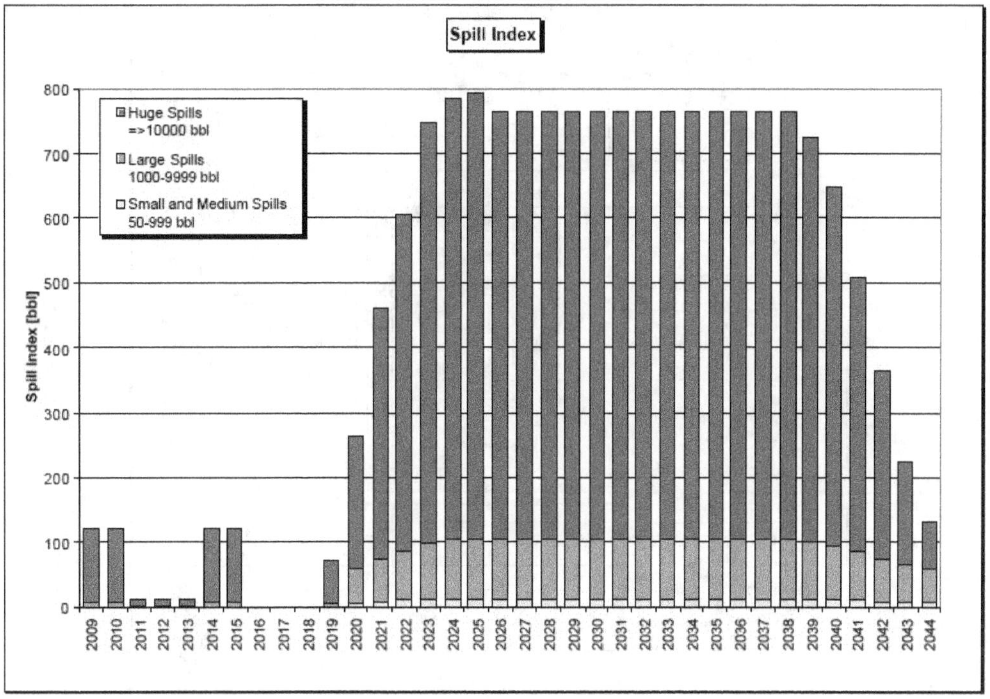

Figure 5.4
Chukchi Sea Spill Index

(Appendix Figure 4.1.03)

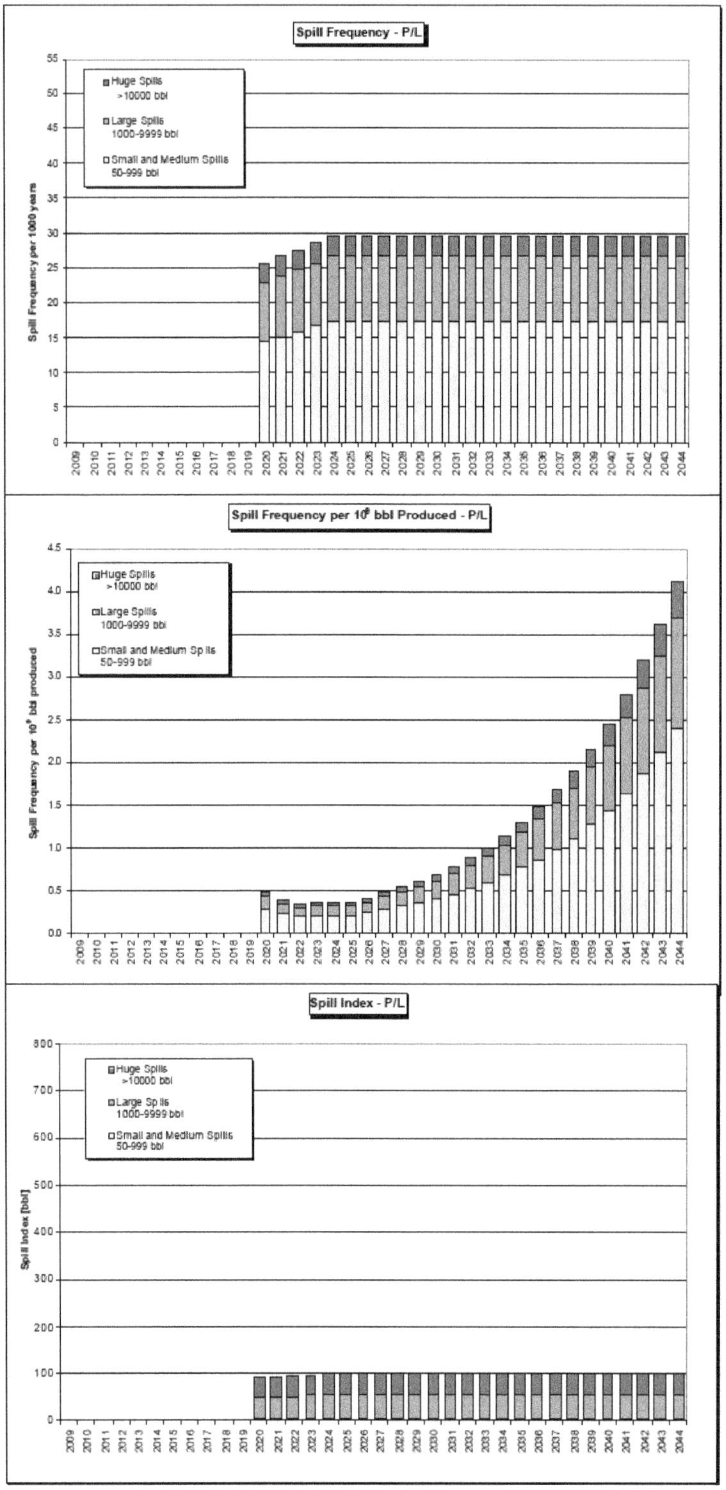

Figure 5.5
Chukchi Sea Spill Indicators – Pipeline
(Appendix Figures 4.1.04, 4.1.05, 4.1.06)

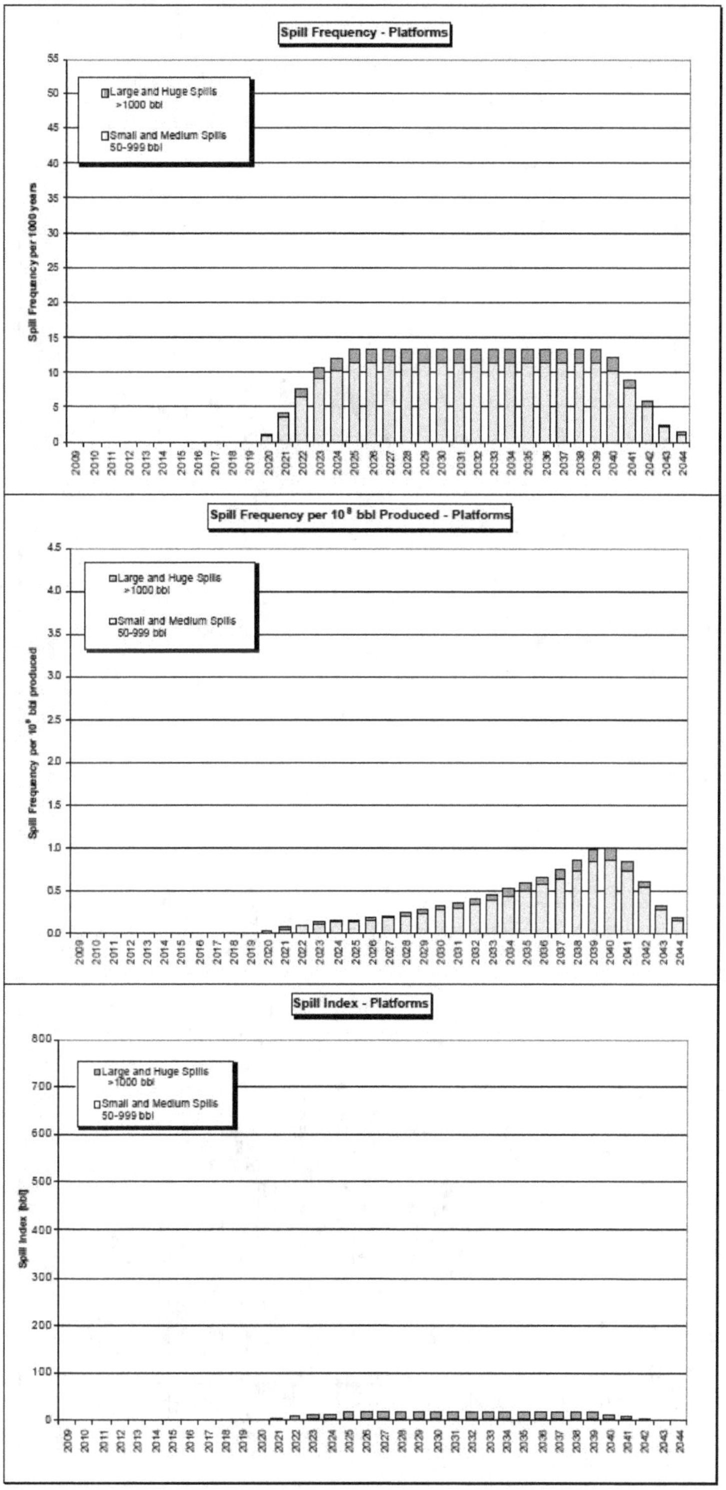

Figure 5.6
Chukchi Sea Spill Indicators – Platforms
(Appendix Figures 4.1.07, 4.1.08, 4.1.09)

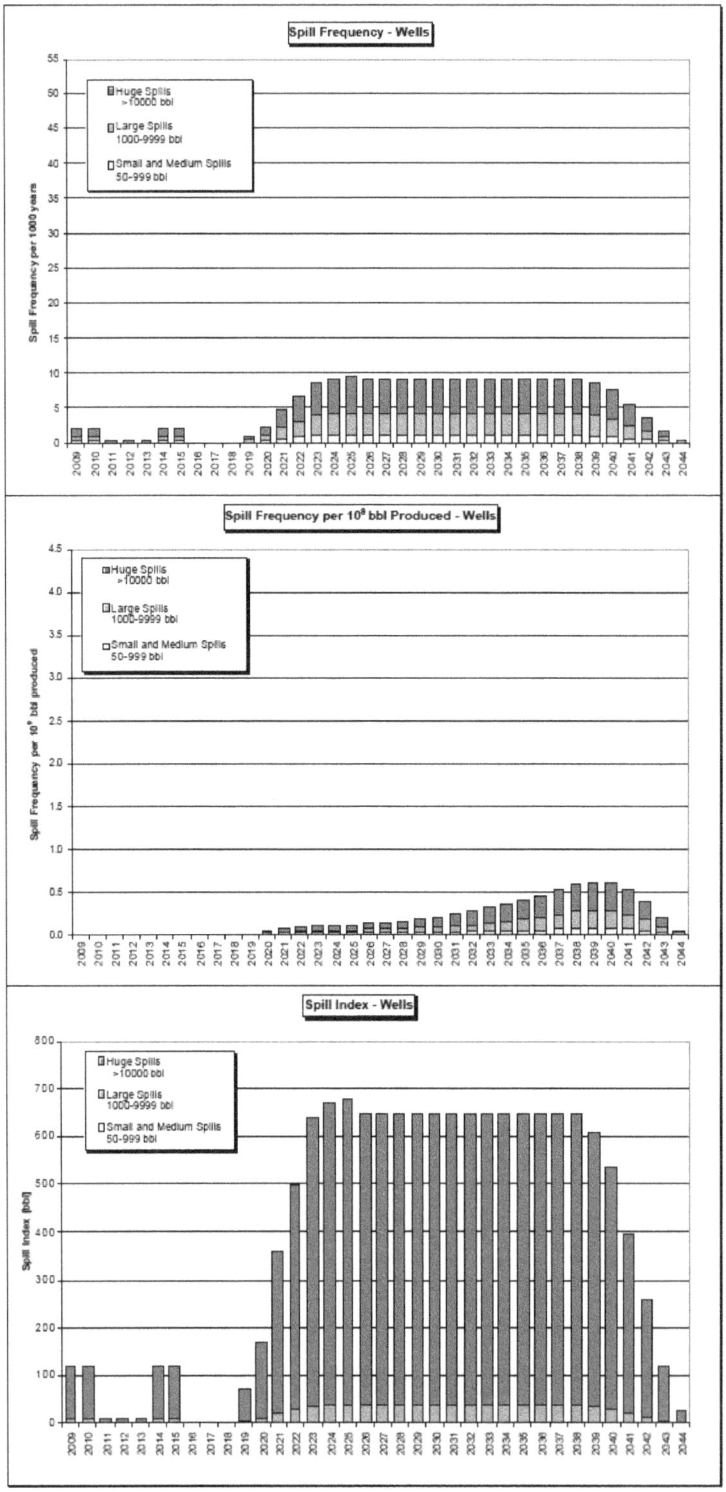

Figure 5.7
Chukchi Sea Spill Indicators – Wells
(Appendix Figures 4.1.10, 4.1.11, 4.1.12)

Table 5.1
Chukchi Sea Year 2024 – Monte Carlo Results *(App. Table 4.1.14)*

Year 2024	Small and Medium Spills 50-999 bbl	Large Spills 1000-9999 bbl	Huge Spills =>10000 bbl	Significant Spills =>1000 bbl	All Spills
	Frequency Spills per 10 years				
Mean =	28.62	13.25	9.00	22.24	50.86
Std Deviation =	9.58	5.70	2.40	6.73	12.77
Variance =	91.791	32.506	5.743	45.293	163.102
Skewness =	0.57	1.10	0.55	0.83	0.54
Kurtosis =	3.24	4.37	3.33	3.82	3.29
Mode =	25.37	11.35	7.34	34.77	46.61
Minimum =	6.959	2.233	2.698	7.478	19.166
5% Perc =	14.801	6.186	5.498	13.138	31.932
10% Perc =	17.026	7.118	6.143	14.641	35.234
15% Perc =	18.780	7.812	6.565	15.653	37.731
20% Perc =	20.186	8.445	6.931	16.547	39.950
25% Perc =	21.421	9.056	7.289	17.285	41.730
30% Perc =	22.786	9.614	7.577	18.136	43.264
35% Perc =	24.053	10.251	7.881	18.906	45.020
40% Perc =	25.298	10.804	8.171	19.616	46.469
45% Perc =	26.372	11.402	8.452	20.381	48.104
50% Perc =	27.659	12.074	8.747	21.222	49.564
55% Perc =	28.854	12.696	9.047	22.026	51.248
60% Perc =	30.179	13.465	9.348	22.850	52.923
65% Perc =	31.604	14.284	9.662	23.826	54.763
70% Perc =	32.981	15.279	10.064	24.871	56.785
75% Perc =	34.572	16.337	10.461	26.089	58.812
80% Perc =	36.468	17.475	10.946	27.449	61.204
85% Perc =	38.630	19.073	11.507	29.141	64.459
90% Perc =	41.498	20.957	12.236	31.377	68.218
95% Perc =	45.695	24.519	13.366	34.951	73.336
Maximum =	71.083	40.789	19.820	54.524	113.299

Year 2024	Small and Medium Spills 50-999 bbl	Large Spills 1000-9999 bbl	Huge Spills =>10000 bbl	Significant Spills =>1000 bbl	All Spills
	Frequency Spills per 10^9 bbl Produced				
Mean =	0.35	0.16	0.11	0.27	0.62
Std Deviation =	0.12	0.07	0.03	0.08	0.16
Variance =	0.014	0.005	0.001	0.007	0.024
Skewness =	0.57	1.10	0.55	0.83	0.54
Kurtosis =	3.24	4.37	3.33	3.82	3.29
Mode =	0.31	0.14	0.09	0.42	0.57
Minimum =	0.085	0.027	0.033	0.091	0.234
5% Perc =	0.180	0.075	0.067	0.160	0.389
10% Perc =	0.208	0.087	0.075	0.179	0.430
15% Perc =	0.229	0.095	0.080	0.191	0.460
20% Perc =	0.246	0.103	0.085	0.202	0.487
25% Perc =	0.261	0.110	0.089	0.211	0.509
30% Perc =	0.278	0.117	0.092	0.221	0.528
35% Perc =	0.293	0.125	0.096	0.231	0.549
40% Perc =	0.309	0.132	0.100	0.239	0.567
45% Perc =	0.322	0.139	0.103	0.249	0.587
50% Perc =	0.337	0.147	0.107	0.259	0.604
55% Perc =	0.352	0.155	0.110	0.269	0.625
60% Perc =	0.368	0.164	0.114	0.279	0.645
65% Perc =	0.385	0.174	0.118	0.291	0.668
70% Perc =	0.402	0.186	0.123	0.303	0.692
75% Perc =	0.422	0.199	0.128	0.318	0.717
80% Perc =	0.445	0.213	0.133	0.335	0.746
85% Perc =	0.471	0.233	0.140	0.355	0.786
90% Perc =	0.506	0.256	0.149	0.383	0.832
95% Perc =	0.557	0.299	0.163	0.426	0.894
Maximum =	0.867	0.497	0.242	0.665	1.382

Year 2024	Small and Medium Spills 50-999 bbl	Large Spills 1000-9999 bbl	Huge Spills =>10000 bbl	Significant Spills =>1000 bbl	All Spills
	Spill Index [bbl]				
Mean =	11.85	90.75	681.33	772.08	783.93
Std Deviation =	6.57	45.99	244.70	251.14	251.46
Variance =	43.199	2115.125	59877.300	63068.880	63234.000
Skewness =	1.21	1.23	0.60	0.59	0.59
Kurtosis =	4.92	5.54	3.45	3.44	3.44
Mode =	13.68	72.01	592.71	385.11	808.80
Minimum =	0.070	7.189	122.468	190.640	201.190
5% Perc =	3.883	31.924	322.006	406.207	416.050
10% Perc =	4.891	40.694	389.326	468.625	481.656
15% Perc =	5.644	47.454	436.771	520.138	530.393
20% Perc =	6.364	52.287	474.957	556.814	568.368
25% Perc =	7.047	57.930	506.613	591.448	603.815
30% Perc =	7.687	62.830	535.962	624.978	636.837
35% Perc =	8.330	67.786	566.772	654.256	666.580
40% Perc =	8.939	72.357	594.537	683.643	695.143
45% Perc =	9.694	77.248	624.378	716.518	728.524
50% Perc =	10.457	82.870	655.379	747.614	760.963
55% Perc =	11.293	88.617	687.216	779.291	791.385
60% Perc =	12.053	94.054	720.446	811.147	823.953
65% Perc =	12.949	99.517	754.067	844.205	856.545
70% Perc =	13.900	106.880	785.081	880.688	891.481
75% Perc =	15.164	113.996	826.945	922.591	933.668
80% Perc =	16.602	123.177	875.826	971.241	983.217
85% Perc =	18.547	135.503	936.725	1030.085	1040.930
90% Perc =	20.683	149.750	1008.444	1114.361	1129.230
95% Perc =	24.617	175.429	1123.291	1221.134	1231.424
Maximum =	54.955	342.292	1813.537	1897.859	1904.195

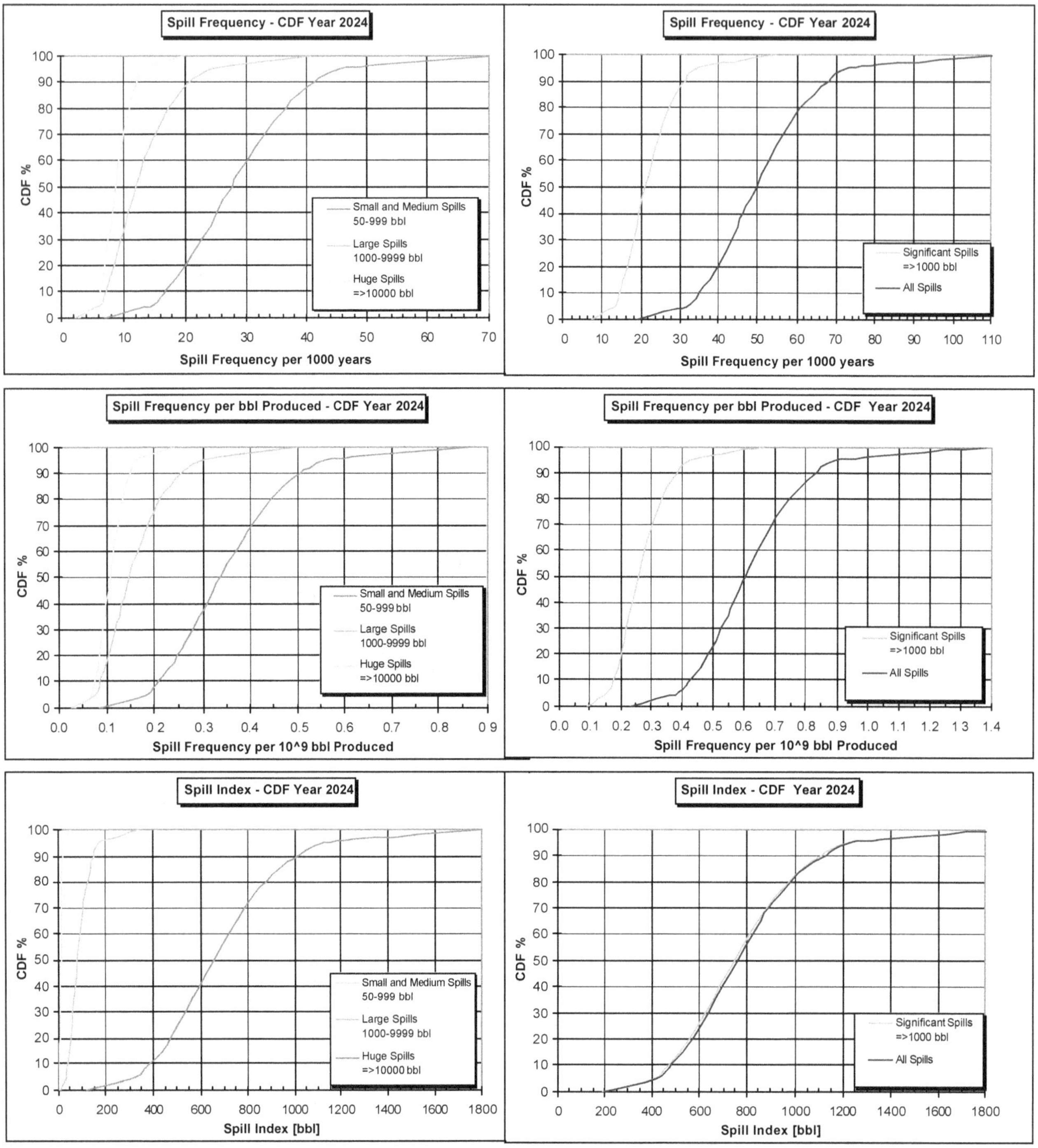

Figure 5.8
Chuckchi Sea Spill Indicator Distributions – Year 2024
(Appendix Figure 4.1.13)

In other words, there is a 50% chance that large and huge spills will occur at a rate of 0.25 per billion bbl or less.

The frequency spill indicator variability can be estimated from the upper (95%) and lower (5%) bound values. For example, for large spill frequency (from Table 5.1), the lower bound (6.186) is 48% of the mean (12.074); the upper bound (24.579), 103% of the mean.

In addition, since the Life of Field (LOF) averages were calculated, results from these are available for each scenario. Only selected ones are given in the text, with the balance given in the appendix. Table 5.2 shows the composition of the spill indicators for the Sale 1 Life of Field average. The composition both by spill size (on the left hand side of the table) and by facility contribution (on the right hand side of the table). The variability of the spill frequencies Life of Field averages is shown in the following figures: Figure 5.9 illustrates the variability of the spill frequency, while Figure 5.10 shows variability of frequency per billion barrels produced.

5.3.2 Comparative Non-Arctic Indicator Assessment

To give an idea of the effect of the frequency variations introduced in Chapter 4, the Chukchi Sea scenario was also modeled utilizing unaltered historical frequencies. That is, no changes to incorporate the Arctic effects were introduced in the spill indicator calculations. Put yet another way, it was assumed that the facilities of the scenario would behave as if they were in the Gulf of Mexico environment rather than in the Arctic environment. Figures 5.11, 5.12, and 5.13 show the total values calculated for each of the three spill indicators. The dark histogram bar on the right side corresponds to the Arctic spill indicator, while that, on the left, corresponds to the computation based on historical frequencies only. Spill frequency in an absolute sense is significantly reduced for the Arctic situation roughly by 32%. The spills per barrel produced are also significantly reduced, as can be seen in Figures 5.14 and 5.15. The spill index (Figure 5.13), because of the disproportionate effect of large spills, shows a reduction of approximately 34%. What the comparison shows is that the Arctic development scenarios can be expected to have a lower oil spill occurrence rate than similar development scenarios in the GOM.

Table 5.2
Composition of Spill Indicators –Life of Field Average *(App. Table 4.1.21)*

Spill Size	Spill Source									
	P/L		Platforms		Wells		Platforms and Wells		All	
	LOF Average - Spill Frequency per 10^3 years									
Small and Medium Spills 50-999 bbl	11.854	58%	6.296	86%	0.599	11%	6.895	54%	18.750	57%
Large Spills 1000-9999 bbl	6.404	32%	0.533	7%	1.798	33%	2.331	18%	8.735	26%
Huge Spills =>10000 bbl	2.042	10%	0.533	7%	3.004	56%	3.536	28%	5.578	17%
Significant Spills =>1000 bbl	8.446	42%	1.066	14%	4.802	89%	5.867	46%	14.313	43%
All Spills	**20.301**	**100%**	**7.362**	**100%**	**5.401**	**100%**	**12.763**	**100%**	**33.063**	**100%**
	LOF Average - Spill Frequency per 10^9 bbl produced									
Small and Medium Spills 50-999 bbl	0.427	58%	0.227	86%	0.022	11%	0.248	54%	0.675	57%
Large Spills 1000-9999 bbl	0.230	32%	0.019	7%	0.065	33%	0.084	18%	0.314	26%
Huge Spills =>10000 bbl	0.073	10%	0.019	7%	0.108	56%	0.127	28%	0.201	17%
Significant Spills =>1000 bbl	0.304	42%	0.038	14%	0.173	89%	0.211	46%	0.515	43%
All Spills	**0.730**	**100%**	**0.265**	**100%**	**0.194**	**100%**	**0.459**	**100%**	**1.190**	**100%**
	LOF Average - Spill Index [bbl]									
Small and Medium Spills 50-999 bbl	5	7%	3	32%	0	0%	3	1%	8	2%
Large Spills 1000-9999 bbl	33	48%	3	34%	22	6%	25	6%	58	13%
Huge Spills =>10000 bbl	31	46%	3	34%	365	94%	368	93%	399	86%
Significant Spills =>1000 bbl	65	93%	6	68%	387	100%	393	99%	457	98%
All Spills	**69**	**100%**	**9**	**100%**	**387**	**100%**	**396**	**100%**	**465**	**100%**

Spill Source	Spill Size									
	S+M 50-999 bbl		Large 1000-9999 bbl		Huge =>10000 bbl		Significant =>1000 bbl		All Spills	
	LOF Average - Spill Frequency per 10^3 years									
P/L	11.854	63%	6.404	73%	2.042	37%	8.446	59%	20.301	61%
Platforms	6.296	34%	0.533	6%	0.533	10%	1.066	7%	7.362	22%
Wells	0.599	3%	1.798	21%	3.004	54%	4.802	34%	5.401	16%
Platforms and Wells	6.895	37%	2.331	27%	3.536	63%	5.867	41%	12.763	39%
All	**18.750**	**100%**	**8.735**	**100%**	**5.578**	**100%**	**14.313**	**100%**	**33.063**	**100%**
	LOF Average - Spill Frequency per 10^9 bbl produced									
P/L	0.427	63%	0.230	73%	0.073	37%	0.304	59%	0.730	61%
Platforms	0.227	34%	0.019	6%	0.019	10%	0.038	7%	0.265	22%
Wells	0.022	3%	0.065	21%	0.108	54%	0.173	34%	0.194	16%
Platforms and Wells	0.248	37%	0.084	27%	0.127	63%	0.211	41%	0.459	39%
All	**0.675**	**100%**	**0.314**	**100%**	**0.201**	**100%**	**0.515**	**100%**	**1.190**	**100%**
	LOF Average - Spill Index [bbl]									
P/L	5	59%	33	57%	31	8%	65	14%	69	15%
Platforms	3	37%	3	5%	3	1%	6	1%	9	2%
Wells	0	4%	22	38%	365	91%	387	85%	387	83%
Platforms and Wells	3	41%	25	43%	368	92%	393	86%	396	85%
All	**8**	**100%**	**58**	**100%**	**399**	**100%**	**457**	**100%**	**465**	**100%**

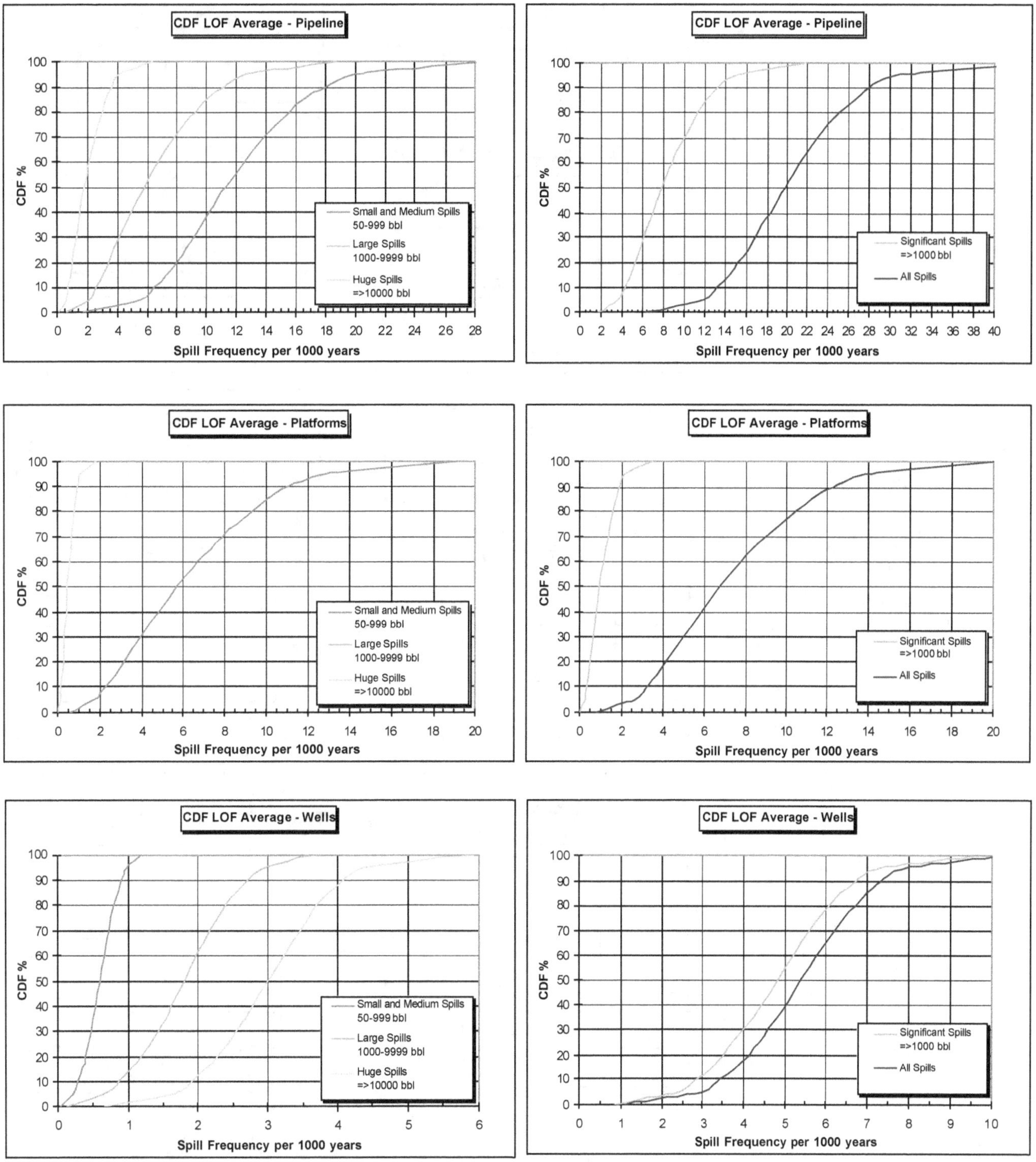

Figure 5.9
Chukchi Sea Life of Field Average Spill Frequency
(Appendix Figure 4.1.14)

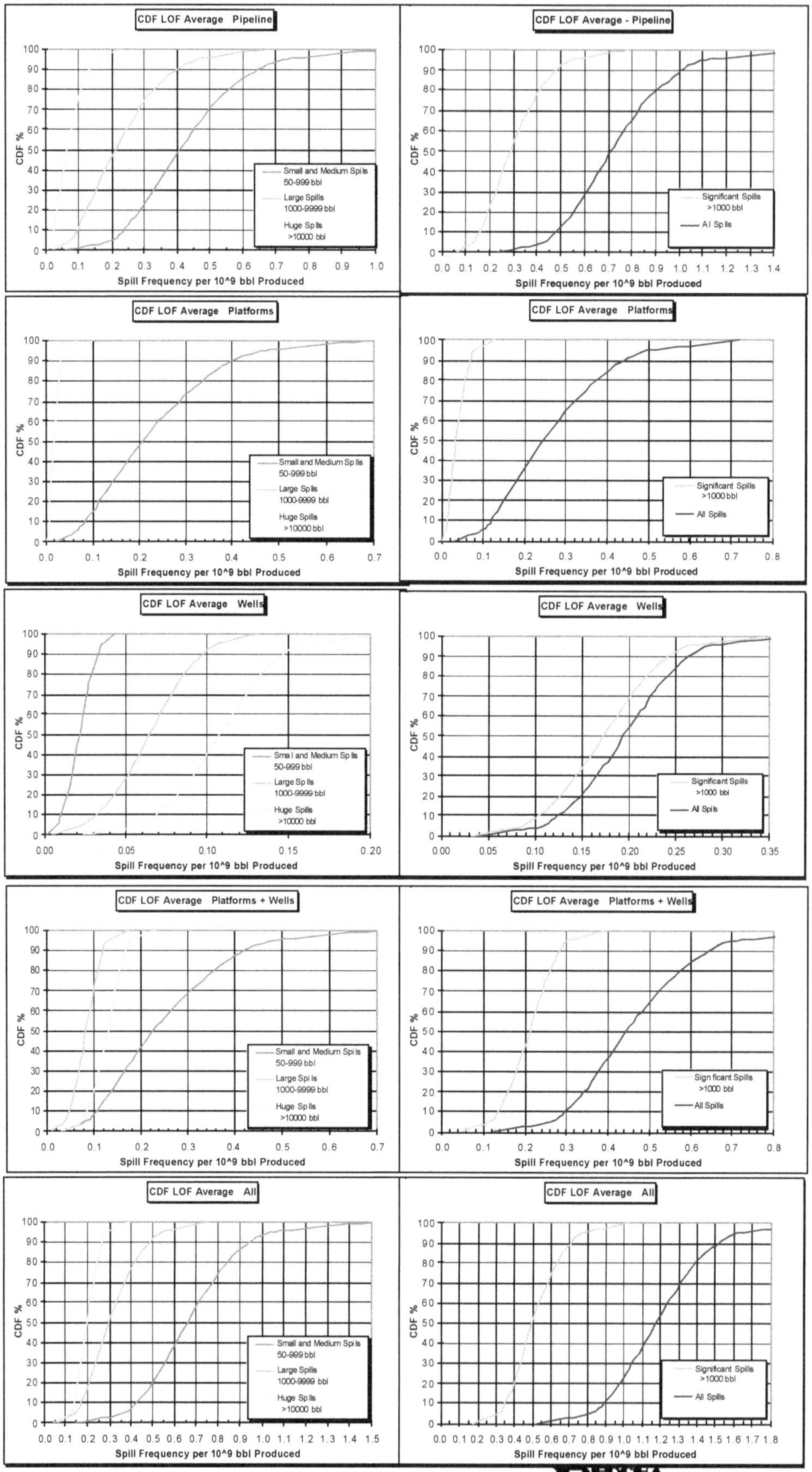

Figure 5.10
Chukchi Sea Life of Field Average Spills per Barrel Produced
(Appendix Figure 4.1.15)

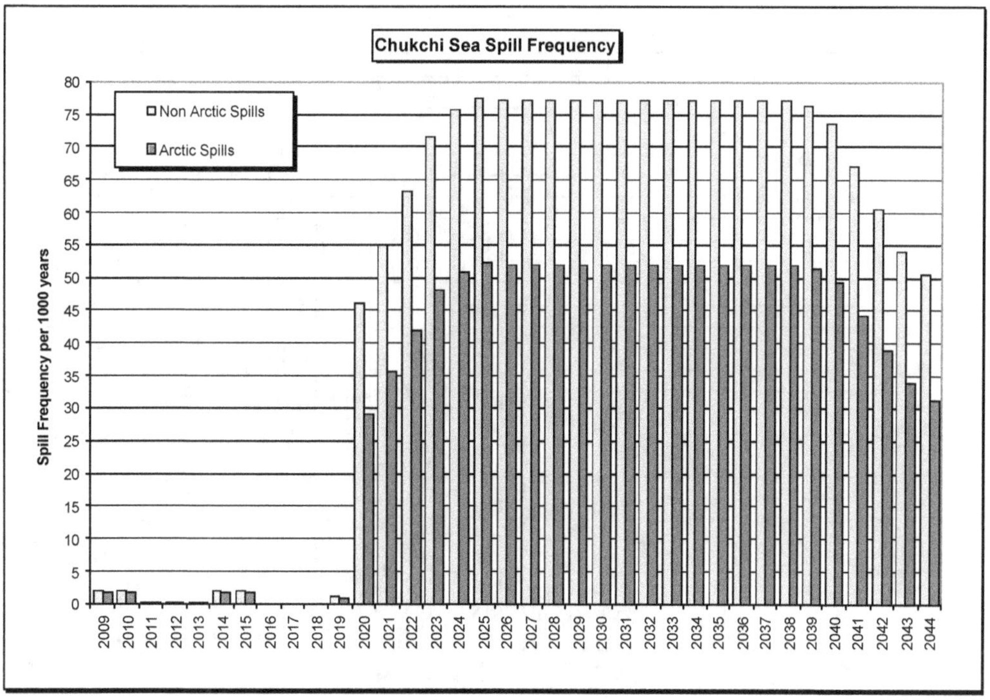

Figure 5.11
Chukchi Sea Spill Frequency – Arctic and Non-Arctic
(Appendix Figure 5.3)

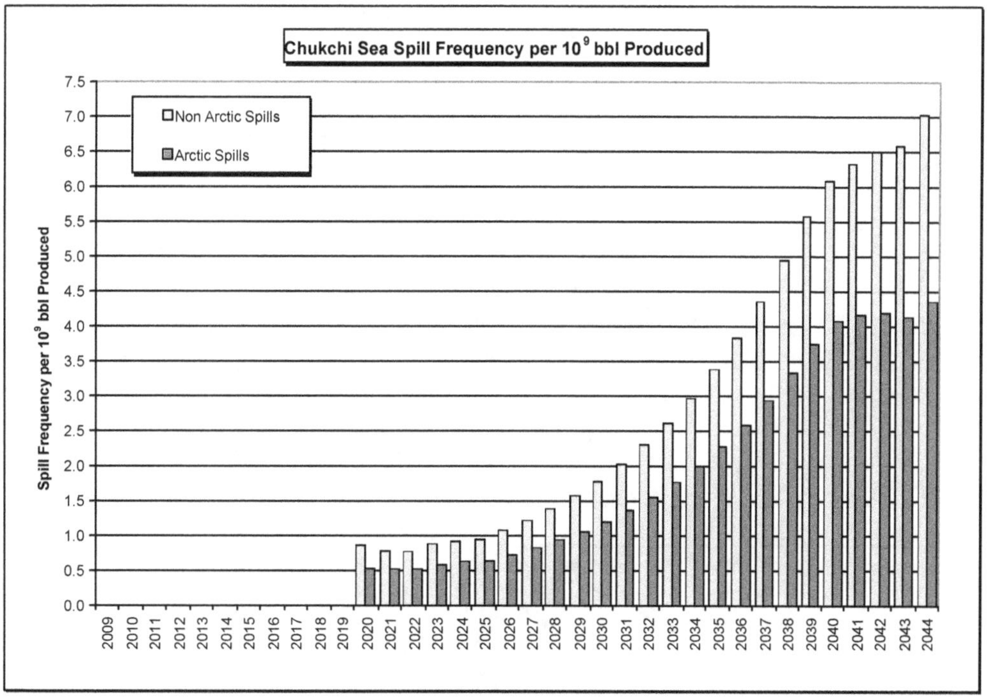

Figure 5.12
Chukchi Sea Spill Frequency per 10^9 Barrels Produced – Arctic and Non-Arctic
(Appendix Figure 5.4)

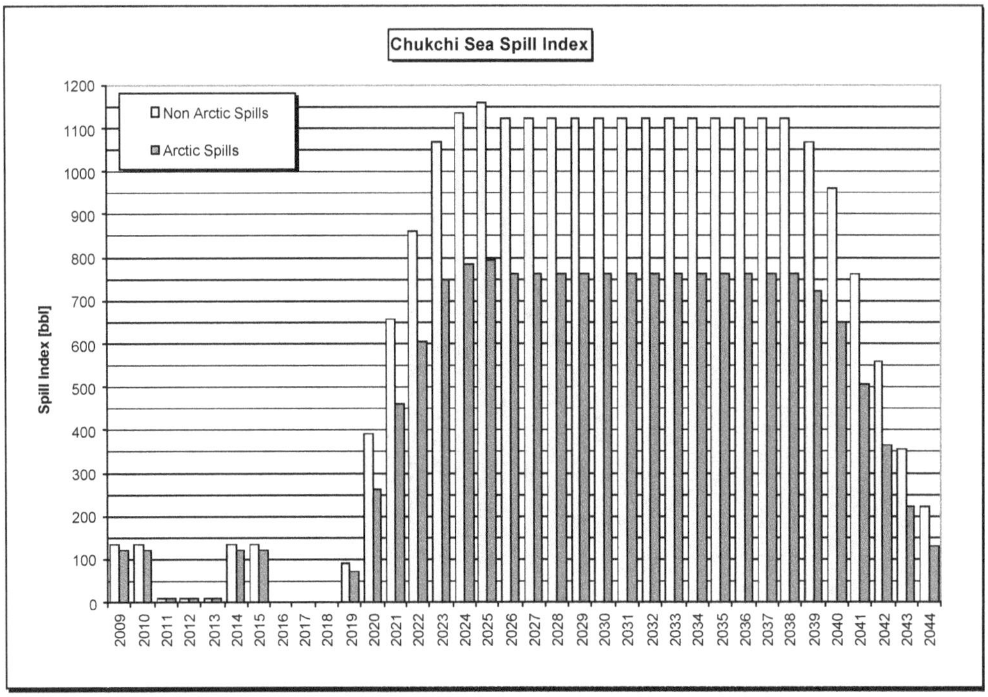

Figure 5.13
Chukchi Sea Spill Index – Arctic and Non-Arctic
(Appendix Figure 5.5)

Table 5.3
Summary of Life of Field Average Spill Indicators by Spill Source and Size
(App Table 5.1)

Spill Indicators LOF Average	Chukchi Sea			Chukchi Sea - Non Arctic		
	Spill Frequency per 10^3 years	Spill Frequency per 10^9 bbl produced	Spill Index [bbl]	Spill Frequency per 10^3 years	Spill Frequency per 10^9 bbl produced	Spill Index [bbl]
Small and Medium Spills 50-999 bbl	18.750	0.675	8	26.111	0.940	11
	57%	**57%**	**2%**	**53%**	**53%**	**2%**
Large Spills 1000-9999 bbl	8.735	0.314	58	14.808	0.533	95
	26%	**26%**	**13%**	**30%**	**30%**	**14%**
Huge Spills =>10000 bbl	5.578	0.201	399	8.593	0.309	574
	17%	**17%**	**86%**	**17%**	**17%**	**84%**
Significant Spills =>1000 bbl	14.313	0.515	458	23.401	0.842	669
	43%	**43%**	**98%**	**47%**	**47%**	**98%**
All Spills	33.063	1.190	465	49.512	1.782	680
	100%	**100%**	**100%**	**100%**	**100%**	**100%**
Pipeline Spills	20.301	0.730	69	33.248	1.196	125
	61%	**61%**	**15%**	**67%**	**67%**	**18%**
Platform Spills	7.362	0.265	9	8.668	0.312	10
	22%	**22%**	**2%**	**18%**	**18%**	**2%**
Well Spills	5.401	0.194	387	7.595	0.273	544
	16%	**16%**	**83%**	**15%**	**15%**	**80%**
Platform and Well Spills	12.763	0.459	396	16.264	0.585	554
	39%	**39%**	**85%**	**33%**	**33%**	**82%**
All Spills	33.063	1.190	465	49.512	1.782	680
	100%	**100%**	**100%**	**100%**	**100%**	**100%**

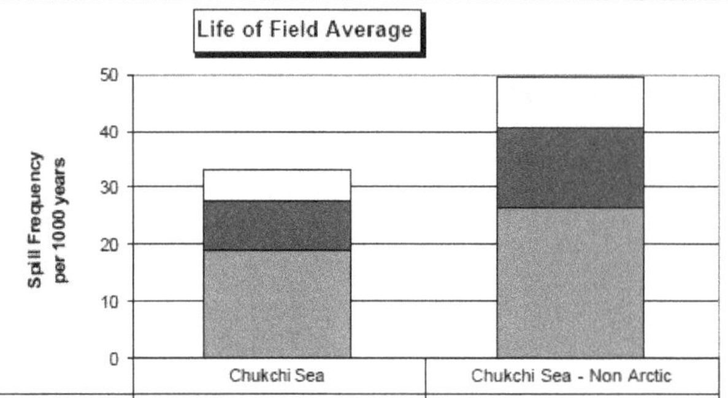

	Chukchi Sea	Chukchi Sea - Non Arctic
Huge Spills =>10000 bbl	5.578	8.593
Large Spills 1000-9999 bbl	8.735	14 808
Small and Medium Spills 50-999 bbl	18.750	26.111

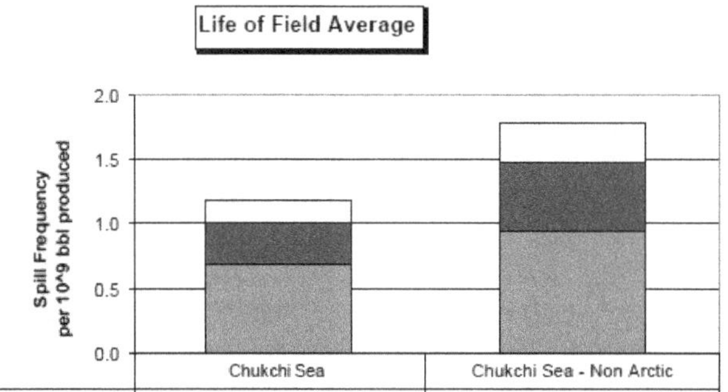

	Chukchi Sea	Chukchi Sea - Non Arctic
Huge Spills =>10000 bbl	0.201	0.309
Large Spills 1000-9999 bbl	0.314	0.533
Small and Medium Spills 50-999 bbl	0.675	0.940

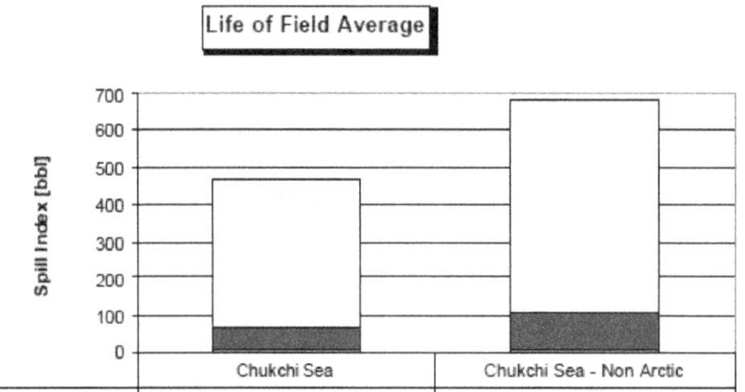

	Chukchi Sea	Chukchi Sea - Non Arctic
Huge Spills =>10000 bbl	399	574
Large Spills 1000-9999 bbl	58	95
Small and Medium Spills 50-999 bbl	8	11

Figure 5.14
Life of Field Spill Indicators – By Spill Size
(Appendix Figure 5.1)

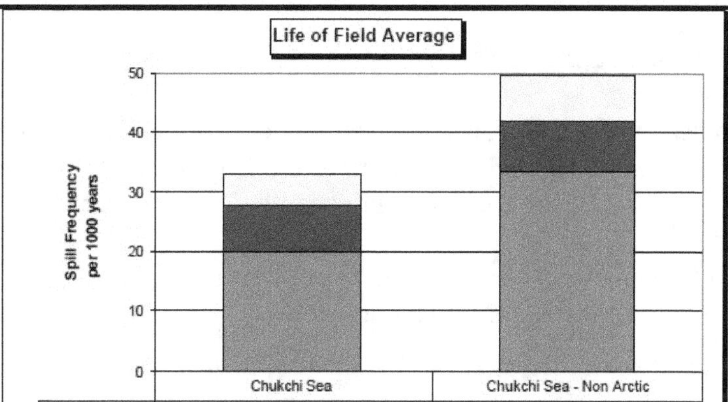

	Chukchi Sea	Chukchi Sea - Non Arctic
Well Spills	5.401	7 595
Platform Spills	7 362	8 668
Pipeline Spills	20.301	33.248

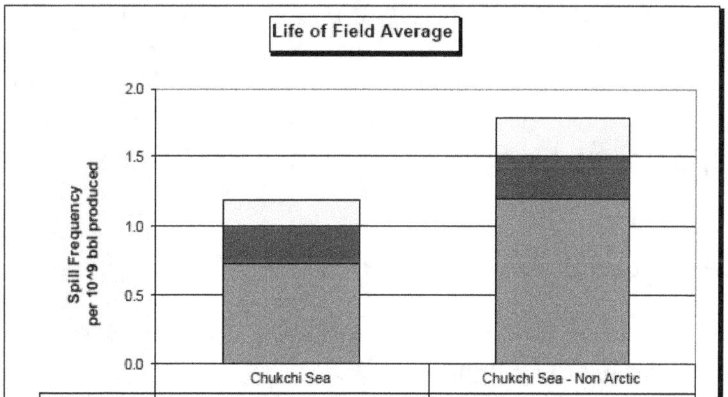

	Chukchi Sea	Chukchi Sea - Non Arctic
Well Spills	0.194	0.273
Platform Spills	0.265	0.312
Pipeline Spills	0.730	1.196

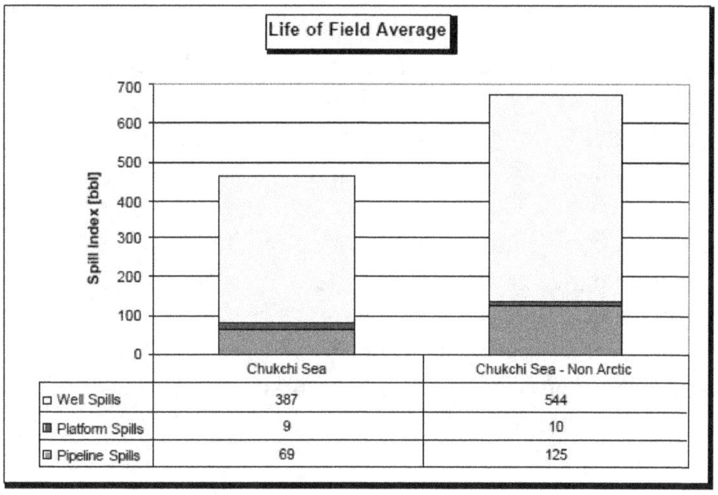

	Chukchi Sea	Chukchi Sea - Non Arctic
Well Spills	387	544
Platform Spills	9	10
Pipeline Spills	69	125

Figure 5.15
Life of Field Spill Indicators – By Source Composition
(Appendix Figure 5.2)

5.4 Summary of Representative Oil Spill Occurrence Indicator Results

How do spill indicators for the Chukchi scenario and for its non-Arctic counterpart vary by spill size and location? Table 5.3 summarizes the Life of Field average spill indicator values by spill source and size. The following can be observed from Table 5.3.

- Spill frequency per year and per barrel-year decreases significantly with increasing spill size for all scenarios.
- The spill index increases significantly with spill size for both scenarios.
- All non-Arctic scenario spill indicators are greater than their Arctic counterparts. Non-Arctic spill indicators are approximately 30% greater.

How do the spill indicators vary by facility type for representative scenarios? The contributions of spill indicators by facility have been summarized by representative scenario years, again, in Table 5.3 and also in Figure 5.15. Table 5.3 and Figure 5.15 give the component contributions, in absolute value and percent, for each of the main facility types; namely, pipelines (P/L), platforms, and wells. The following may be noted from Table 5.3:

- Pipelines contribute the most (61%) to the two spill frequency indicators.
- Platforms are next in relative contribution to spill frequencies (22%) and least in contribution to spill index (2%).
- Wells are by far (at 83%) the highest contributors to spill index, while platforms and wells together are responsible for a 82% contribution to the spill index.
- It can be concluded that pipelines are likely to have the most, but smaller spills, while wells will have the least number, but largest spills. Platforms will be in between, with a tendency towards more spills than wells, but less or about the same number as platforms.

Figures 5.16 and 5.17 show relative contributions by facility and spill size to the maximum production year 2024 and Life of Field average spill indicators, respectively. Although Life of Field average absolute values are significantly smaller than the maximum production year values, the proportional contributions by spill facility source and spill size are almost identical. In Figures 5.16 and 5.17, "TOTAL" designates the sum of the spill indicators for all spill sizes and facility types.

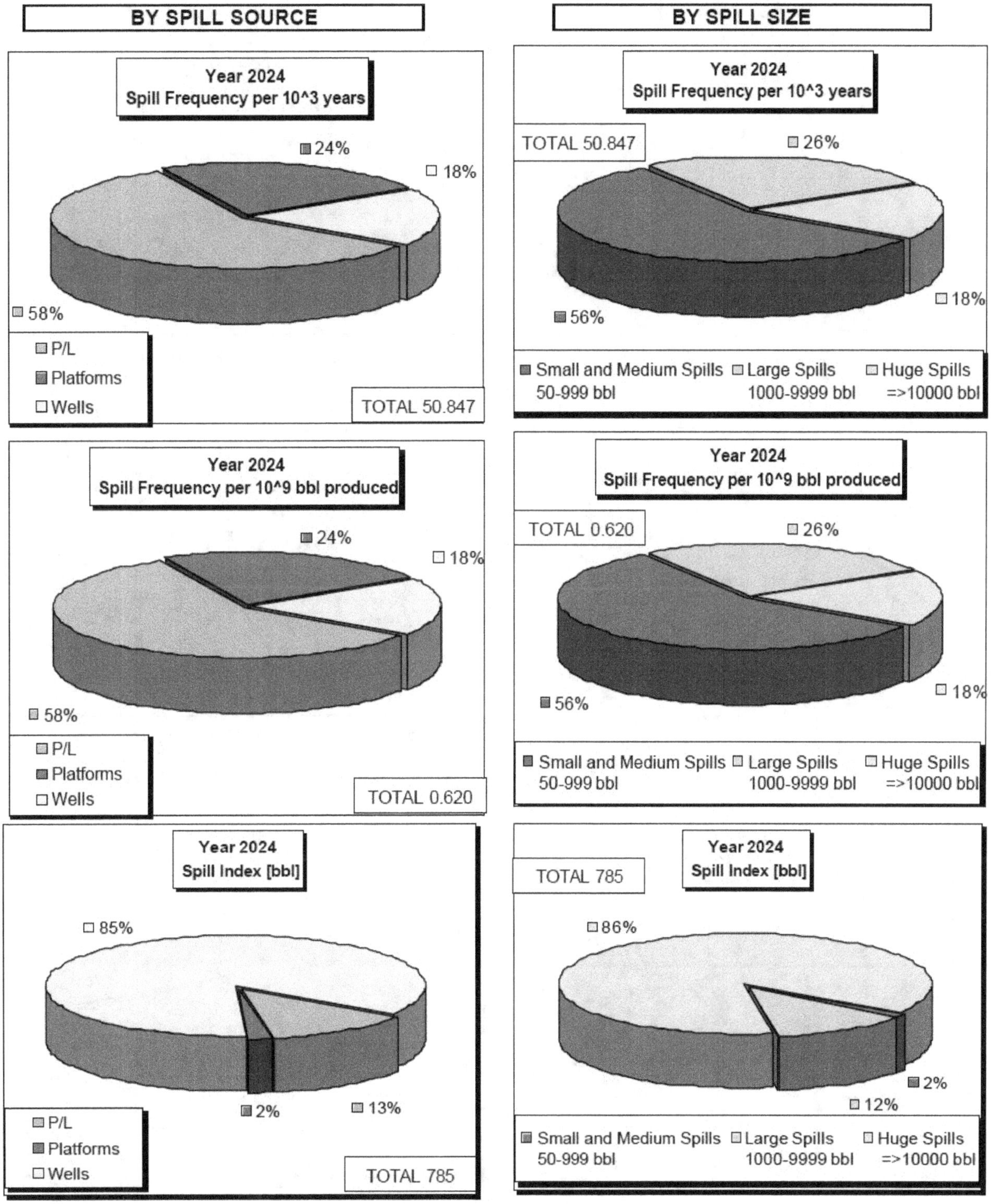
BY SPILL SOURCE
BY SPILL SIZE
Year 2024
Spill Frequency per 10^3 years
24%
18%
58%
P/L
Platforms
Wells
TOTAL 50.847
Year 2024
Spill Frequency per 10^3 years
TOTAL 50.847
26%
18%
56%
Small and Medium Spills 50-999 bbl
Large Spills 1000-9999 bbl
Huge Spills =>10000 bbl
Year 2024
Spill Frequency per 10^9 bbl produced
24%
18%
58%
P/L
Platforms
Wells
TOTAL 0.620
Year 2024
Spill Frequency per 10^9 bbl produced
TOTAL 0.620
26%
18%
56%
Small and Medium Spills 50-999 bbl
Large Spills 1000-9999 bbl
Huge Spills =>10000 bbl
Year 2024
Spill Index [bbl]
85%
2%
13%
P/L
Platforms
Wells
TOTAL 785
TOTAL 785
Year 2024
Spill Index [bbl]
86%
2%
12%
Small and Medium Spills 50-999 bbl
Large Spills 1000-9999 bbl
Huge Spills =>10000 bbl

Figure 5.16
Chukchi Sea – Year 2024 – Spill Indicator Composition by Source and Spill Size
(Appendix Figure 4.1.17)

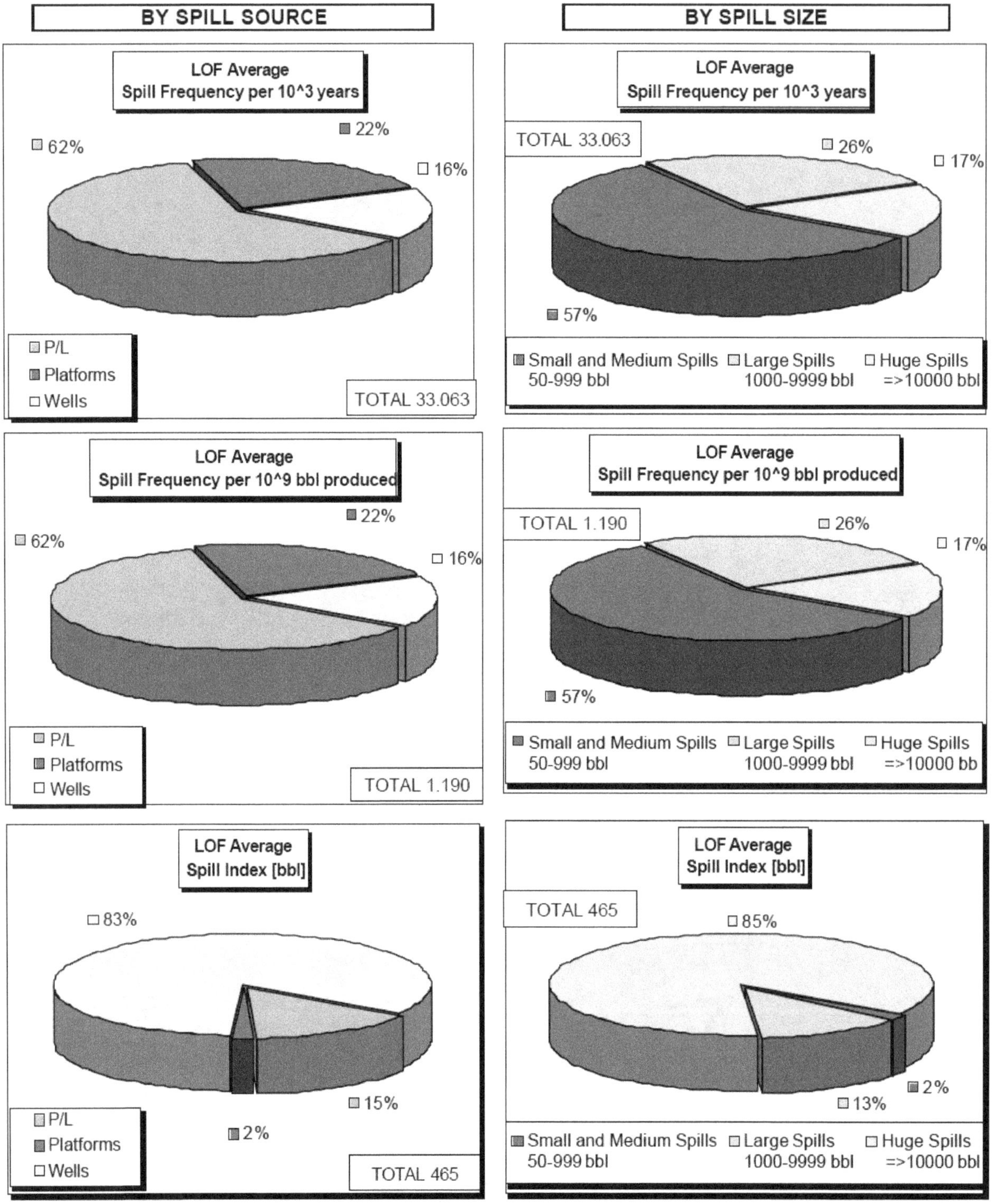
BY SPILL SOURCE
BY SPILL SIZE
LOF Average
Spill Frequency per 10^3 years
62%
22%
16%
P/L
Platforms
Wells
TOTAL 33.063
LOF Average
Spill Frequency per 10^3 years
TOTAL 33.063
26%
17%
57%
Small and Medium Spills 50-999 bbl
Large Spills 1000-9999 bbl
Huge Spills =>10000 bbl
LOF Average
Spill Frequency per 10^9 bbl produced
62%
22%
16%
P/L
Platforms
Wells
TOTAL 1.190
LOF Average
Spill Frequency per 10^9 bbl produced
TOTAL 1.190
26%
17%
57%
Small and Medium Spills 50-999 bbl
Large Spills 1000-9999 bbl
Huge Spills =>10000 bb
LOF Average
Spill Index [bbl]
83%
15%
2%
P/L
Platforms
Wells
TOTAL 465
LOF Average
Spill Index [bbl]
TOTAL 465
85%
2%
13%
Small and Medium Spills 50-999 bbl
Large Spills 1000-9999 bbl
Huge Spills =>10000 bbl

Figure 5.17
Chukchi Sea – Life of Field Average Spill Indicator Composition by Source and Spill Size
(Appendix Figure 4.1.18)

Figures 5.18, 5.19, and 5.20 show the Cumulative Distribution Functions (CDF) for the Chukchi Sea Life of Field average spill indicators. The variability of these indicators is fairly representative of the trends in variability for spill indicators for all sales and locations studied. Generally, the following can be observed from the figures:

- The variance of the frequency spill indicators (Figures 5.18 and 5.19) decreases as spill size increases for pipelines and platforms. In other words, small and medium spills illustrate the largest variability; huge spills show the least variability for these facilities.
- The opposite occurs for wells.
- The variability of the spill index (Figure 5.20) shows the opposite trend for pipelines and platforms.

The Cumulative Distribution Functions contain extensive information on the statistical properties of the spill indicators. For example, from Figure 5.18, it can be seen, for all significant spills, that the Life of Field average mean (50%) value of 14 (spills per 1,000 years) ranges between 23 and 7 at the upper and lower 95% confidence intervals. A similar percentage variation is shown for the Life of Field average spill frequency per barrel produced in Figure 5.19. The spill index variability shown in Figure 5.20 is proportionally higher. For example, in Figure 5.20, the mean value of the significant spills index of 450 per billion barrels produced ranges from 250 to 700.

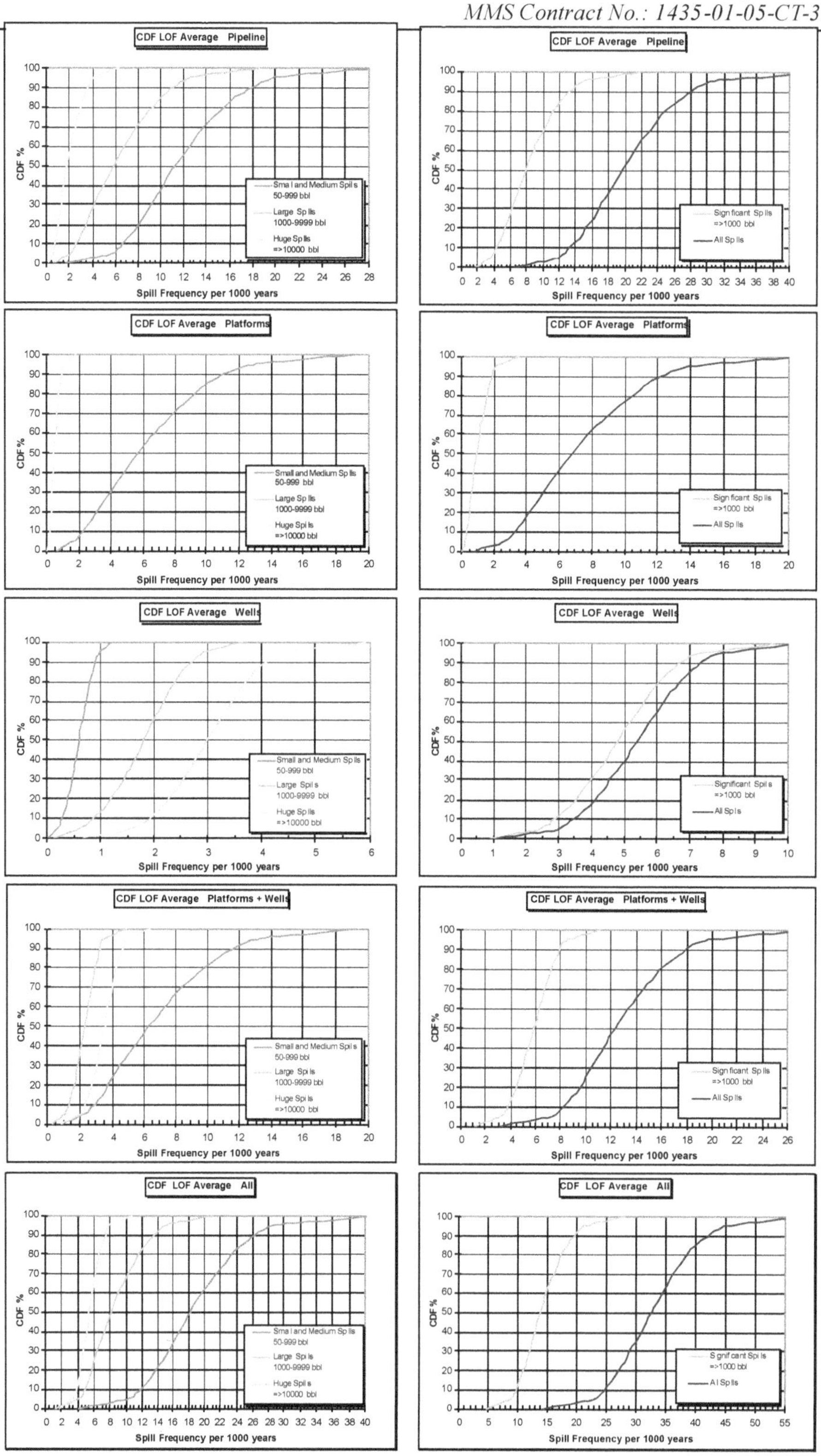

Figure 5.18
Chukchi Sea Life of Field Average Spill Frequency – CDF
(Appendix Figure 4.1.14)

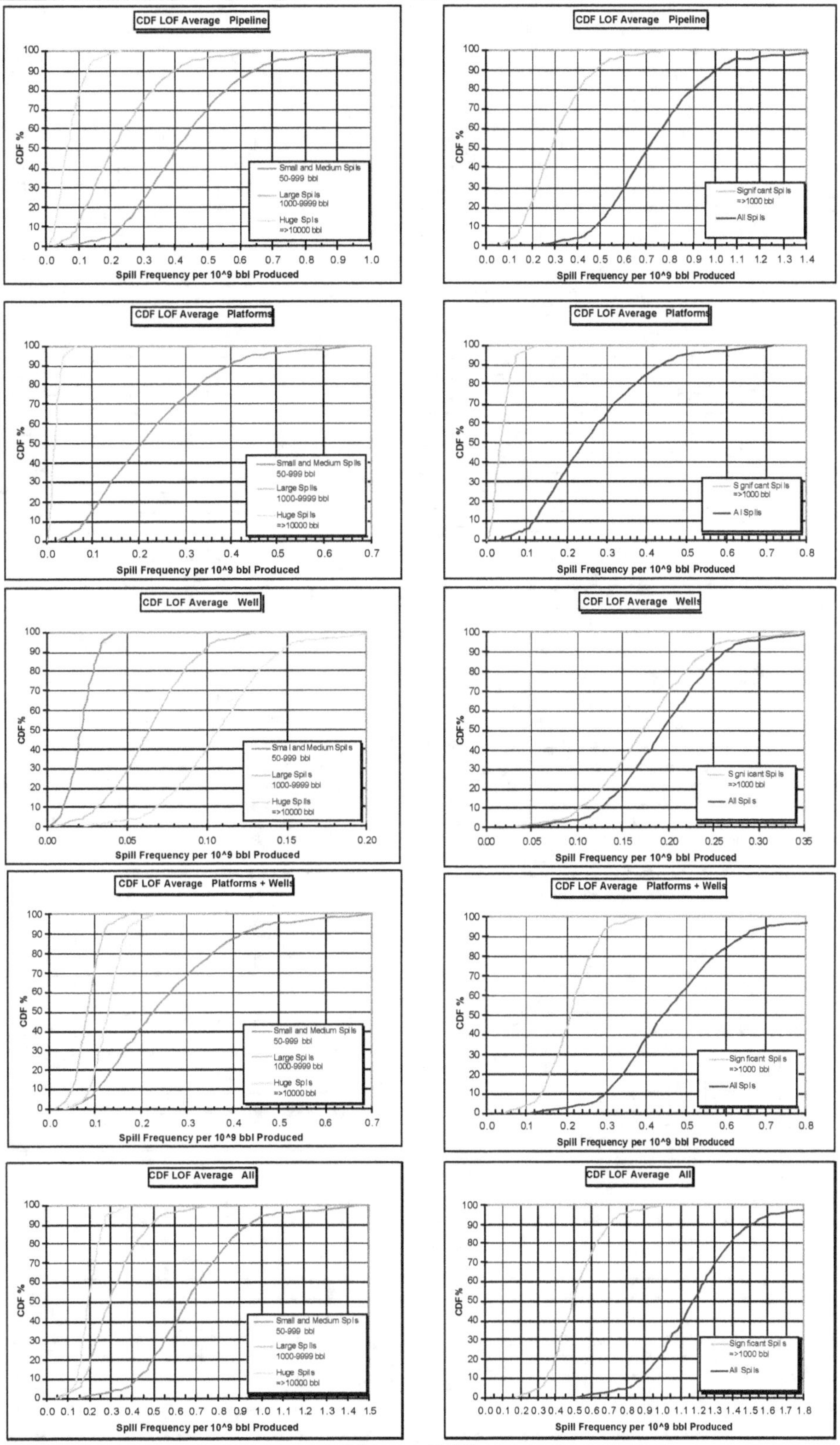

Figure 5.19
Chukchi Sea Life of Field Average Spill Frequency per Barrel Produced – CDF
(Appendix Figure 4.1.15)

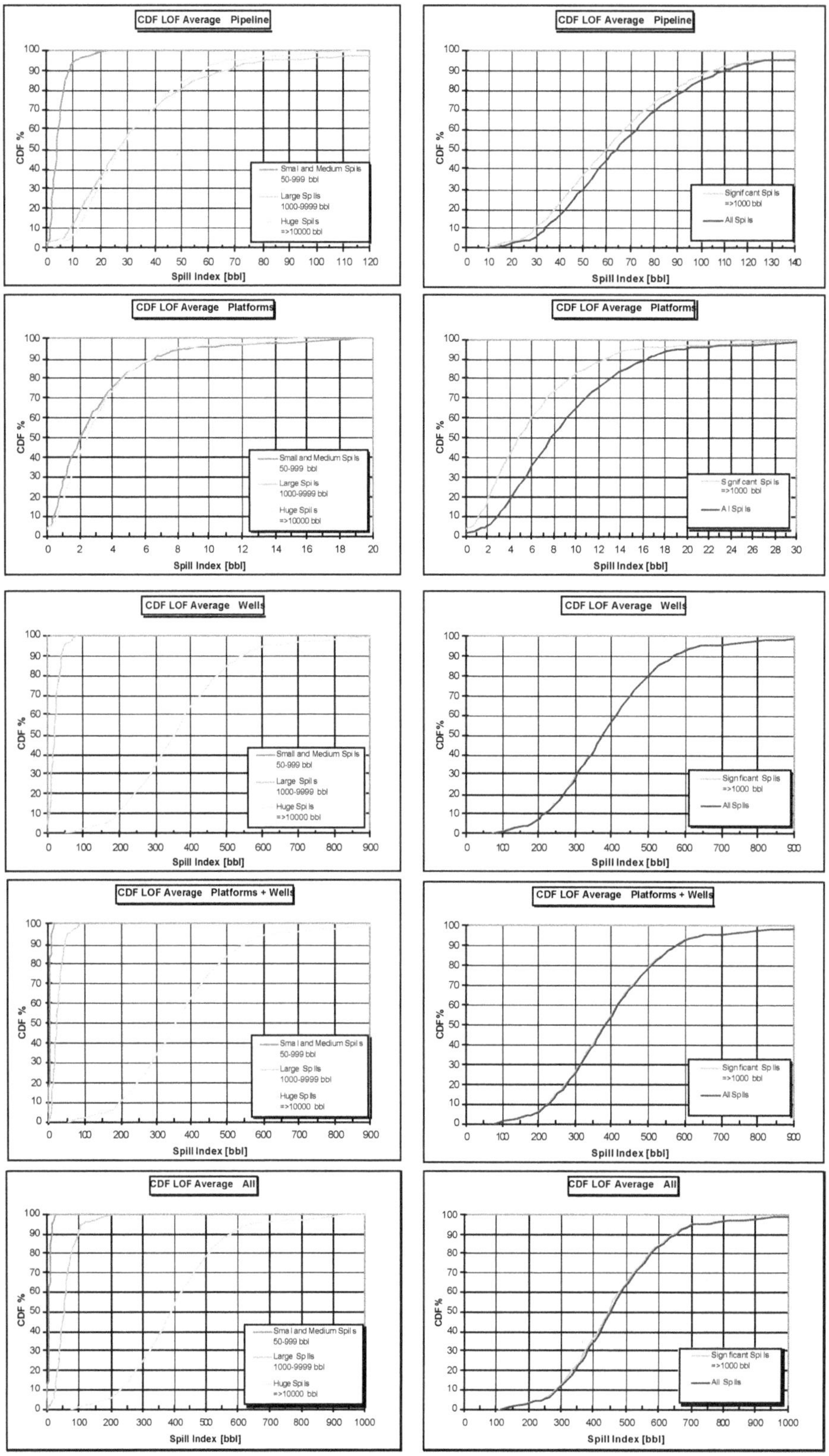

Figure 5.20
Chukchi Sea Life of Field Average Spill Index (bbl) – CDF
(Appendix Figure 4.1.16)

CHAPTER 6

CONCLUSIONS AND RECOMMENDATIONS

6.1 Conclusions

6.1.1 General Conclusions

Oil spill occurrence indicators were quantified for future offshore development scenarios in the Chukchi Sea in the area of MMS jurisdiction. The quantification included the consideration of the variability of historical and future scenario data, as well as that of Arctic effects in predicting oil spill occurrence indicators. Consideration of the variability of all input data yields both higher variability and a higher expected value of the spill occurrence indicators. The three types of spill occurrence indicators were: annual oil spill frequency, annual oil spill frequency per billion barrels produced, and annual spill index – and, additionally, the life of field averages for each of these three oil spill indicators were assessed.

6.1.2 Oil Spill Occurrence Indicators by Spill Size

How do spill indicators for the different scenarios and for their non-Arctic counterparts vary by spill size and source? Table 6.1 summarizes the Life of Field (LOF) average spill indicator values. Figure 6.1 illustrates these. The following can be observed from Table 6.1.

- Spill frequency per year and per barrel-year decreases significantly with increasing spill size for all scenarios.
- The spill index increases significantly with spill size for both scenarios.
- All non-Arctic scenario spill indicators are greater than their Arctic counterparts. Non-Arctic spill indicators are approximately 30% greater.

Table 6.1
Summary of Life of Field Average Spill Indicators by Spill Source and Size

Spill Indicators LOF Average	Chukchi Sea			Chukchi Sea - Non Arctic		
	Spill Frequency per 10^3 years	Spill Frequency per 10^9 bbl produced	Spill Index [bbl]	Spill Frequency per 10^3 years	Spill Frequency per 10^9 bbl produced	Spill Index [bbl]
Small and Medium Spills 50-999 bbl	18.750	0.675	8	26.111	0.940	11
	57%	**57%**	**2%**	**53%**	**53%**	**2%**
Large Spills 1000-9999 bbl	8.735	0.314	58	14.808	0.533	95
	26%	**26%**	**13%**	**30%**	**30%**	**14%**
Huge Spills =>10000 bbl	5.578	0.201	399	8.593	0.309	574
	17%	**17%**	**86%**	**17%**	**17%**	**84%**
Significant Spills =>1000 bbl	14.313	0.515	458	23.401	0.842	669
	43%	**43%**	**98%**	**47%**	**47%**	**98%**
All Spills	33.063	1.190	465	49.512	1.782	680
	100%	**100%**	**100%**	**100%**	**100%**	**100%**
Pipeline Spills	20.301	0.730	69	33.248	1.196	125
	61%	**61%**	**15%**	**67%**	**67%**	**18%**
Platform Spills	7.362	0.265	9	8.668	0.312	10
	22%	**22%**	**2%**	**18%**	**18%**	**2%**
Well Spills	5.401	0.194	387	7.595	0.273	544
	16%	**16%**	**83%**	**15%**	**15%**	**80%**
Platform and Well Spills	12.763	0.459	396	16.264	0.585	554
	39%	**39%**	**85%**	**33%**	**33%**	**82%**
All Spills	33.063	1.190	465	49.512	1.782	680
	100%	**100%**	**100%**	**100%**	**100%**	**100%**

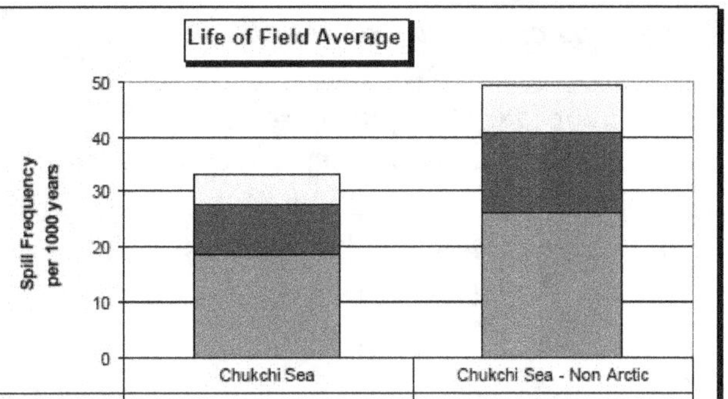

	Chukchi Sea	Chukchi Sea - Non Arctic
Huge Spills =>10000 bbl	5.578	8.593
Large Spills 1000-9999 bbl	8.735	14 808
Small and Medium Spills 50-999 bbl	18.750	26.111

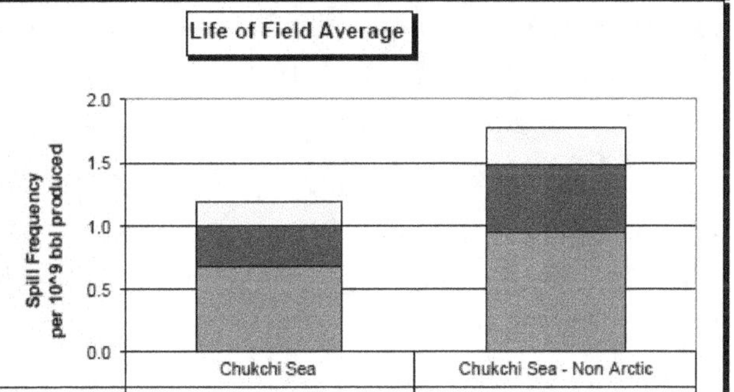

	Chukchi Sea	Chukchi Sea - Non Arctic
Huge Spills =>10000 bbl	0.201	0.309
Large Spills 1000-9999 bbl	0.314	0.533
Small and Medium Spills 50-999 bbl	0.675	0.940

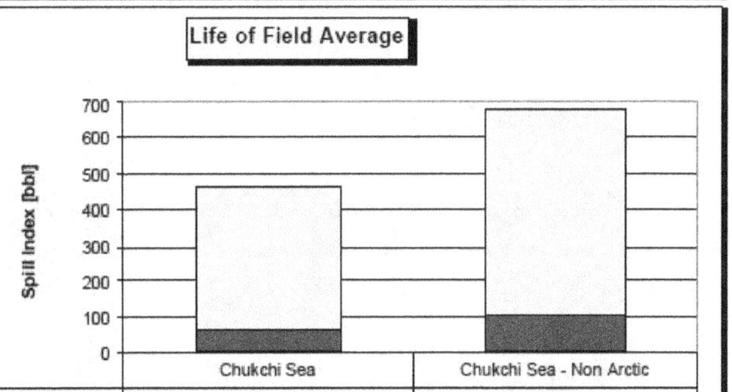

	Chukchi Sea	Chukchi Sea - Non Arctic
Huge Spills =>10000 bbl	399	574
Large Spills 1000-9999 bbl	58	95
Small and Medium Spills 50-999 bbl	8	11

Figure 6.1
Life of Field Spill Indicators – By Spill Size

6.1.3 Oil Spill Occurrence Indicators by Spill Source

How do the spill indicators vary by spill source facility type for representative scenarios? The contributions of spill indicators by source facility have been summarized by Life of Field averages, in Table 6.1 and also in Figure 5.15. Table 6.1 and Figure 5.15 give the component contributions, in absolute value and percent, for each of the main facility types; namely, pipelines (P/L), platforms, and wells. The following may be noted from Table 6.1:

- Pipelines contribute the most (61%) to the two spill frequency indicators.
- Platforms are next in relative contribution to spill frequencies (22%) and least in contribution to spill index (2%).
- Wells are by far (at 83%) the highest contributors to spill index, while platforms and wells together are responsible for a 82% contribution to the spill index.
- It can be concluded that pipelines are likely to have the most, but smaller spills, while wells will have the least number, but largest spills. Platforms will be in between, with a tendency towards more spills than wells, but less or about the same number as platforms.

Figures 5.16 and 5.17 show relative contributions by facility and spill size to the maximum production year 2024 and Life of Field average spill indicators, respectively. Although Life of Field average spill indicator absolute values are significantly smaller than the maximum production year values, the proportional contributions by spill facility source and spill size are almost identical.

6.1.4 Variability of Oil Spill Occurrence Indicators

Figures 5.18, 5.19, and 5.20 show the Cumulative Distribution Functions for each of the Chukchi Sea Life of Field average spill indicators by spill size and source. Generally, the following can be observed from the figures:

- The variance of the frequency spill indicators (Figures 5.18 and 5.19) decreases as spill size increases for pipelines and platforms. In other words, small and medium spills illustrate the largest variability; huge spills show the least variability for these facilities.
- The opposite occurs for wells.
- The variability of the spill index (Figure 5.20) shows the opposite trend for pipelines and platforms.

The Cumulative Distribution Functions contain extensive information on the statistical properties of the spill indicators. For example, from Figure 5.18, it can be seen, for all significant spills, that the Life of Field average mean (50%) value of 14 (spills per 1,000 years) ranges between 23 and 7 at the upper and lower 95% confidence intervals. A similar percentage variation is shown for the Life of Field average spill frequency per barrel produced in Figure 5.19. The spill index variability shown in Figure 5.20 is proportionally higher. For example, in Figure 5.20, the mean value of the significant spills index of 450 per billion barrels produced ranges from 250 to 700.

6.2 Conclusions on the Methodology and its Applicability

An analytical tool for the prediction of oil spill occurrence indicators for systems without history, such as future offshore oil production developments in the Chukchi Sea, has been developed based on the utilization of fault tree methodology. Although the results generated are voluminous, they are essentially transparent, simple, and easy to understand. The analytical tool developed is also quite transparent, very efficient in terms of computer time and input-output capability. In addition, the predictive model is setup so that any input variables can be entered as distributions.

A wealth of information that can be utilized for the optimal planning and regulation of future developments is generated by the analytical tool. Key aspects of the analytical tool capability may be summarized as follows:

- Ability to generate expected and mean values as well as their variability in rigorous numerical statistical format.
- Use of verifiable input data based on MMS or other historical spill data and statistics.
- Ability to independently vary the impacts of different causes on the spill occurrences as well as add new causes such as some of those that may be expected for the Arctic or other new environments.
- Ability to generate spill occurrence indicator characteristics such as annual variations, facility contributions, spill size distributions, and life of field (Life of Field) averages.
- Ability to generate comparative spill occurrence indicators such as those of comparable scenarios in more temperate regions. The model developed provides a basis for estimating each Arctic effect's importance through sensitivity analysis as well as propagation of uncertainties.
- Capability to quantify uncertainties rigorously, together with their measures of variability.

6.3 Limitations of the Methodology and Results

During the work, a number of limitations in the input data, the scenarios, the application of the fault tree methodology, and finally the oil spill occurrence indicators themselves have been identified. These shortcomings are summarized in the following paragraphs.

Two categories of input data were used; namely the historical spill data and the Arctic effect data. Although a verifiable and optimal historical spill data set has been used, the following shortcomings may be noted:

- Gulf of Mexico (OCS) historical data bases were provided by MMS for pipelines and facilities, and were used as a starting point for the fault tree analysis. Although these data are adequate, a broader population base would give more robust statistics. Unfortunately, data from a broader population base, such as the North Sea, do not contain the level of detail provided in the GOM data.

- The Arctic effects include modifications in causes associated with the historical data set as well as additions of spill causes unique to the Arctic environment. Quantification of existing causes for Arctic effects was done in a relative cursory way restricted to engineering judgment.

- Upheaval buckling effect assessments were included on the basis of an educated guess; no engineering analysis was carried out for the assessment of frequencies to be expected for these effects.

- A reproducible but relatively elementary analysis of gouging and scour effects was carried out.

The scenarios are those developed for use in the MMS Alaska OCS Region Environmental Impact Statements for Oil and Gas Lease Sales. As estimated they appear reasonable and were incorporated in the form provided.

- The only shortcoming appears to be that the facility abandonment rate is significantly lower than the rate of decline in production.

The following comments can be made on limitations associated with the indicators that have been generated:

- The indicators have inherited the deficiencies of the input and scenario data noted above.

- The model generating the indicators is fundamentally a linear model which ignores the effects of scale, of time variations such as the learning and wear-out curves (Bathtub curve), and production volume non-linear effects.

6.4 Recommendations

The following recommendations based on the work may be made:

- Continue to utilize the Monte Carlo spill occurrence indicator model for new scenarios to support MMS needs, as it is currently the best predictive spill occurrence model available.

- Utilize the oil spill occurrence indicator model to generate additional model validation information, including direct application to specific non-Arctic scenarios, such as GOM projects, which have an oil spill statistical history.

- Utilize the oil spill occurrence indicator model in a sensitivity mode to identify the importance of different Arctic effect variables introduced to provide a prioritized list of those items having the highest potential impact on Arctic oil spills.

- Generalize the model so that it can be run both in an adjusted expected value and a distributed value (Monte Carlo) form with the intent that expected value form can be utilized without the Monte Carlo add-in for preliminary estimates and sensitivity analyses, while for more comprehensive rigorous studies, the Monte Carlo version can be used.

REFERENCES

1. AIChE, "Guidelines for Chemical Process Quantitative Risk Analysis", 2nd Edition, Center for Chemical Process Safety, NY, 2000.
2. Anderson, Cheryl McMahon, and Robert P. LaBelle, "Update of Comparative Occurrence Rates for Offshore Oil Spills", Spill Science & Technology Bulletin, Vol. 6., No. 5/6, pp. 303-321, 2000.
3. Beaumont, S., "Refinery Construction in Arctic Weather Conditions – Some Construction, Inspection, and Corrosion Concerns", in Material Performance, Vol. 26:8, pp 53-56, 01 August 1987.
4. Bercha F.G., "Special Problems in Pipeline Risk Assessment", Proceedings of IPC 2000, International Pipeline Conference, Calgary, AB, October 1-5, 2000.
5. Bercha, F.G., A.C. Churcher, and M. Cerovšek, "Escape, Evacuation, and Rescue Modeling for Frontier Offshore Installations", Offshore Technology Conference, Houston, Texas, USA, 2000.
6. Bercha, F.G., and M. Cerovšek, Large Arctic Offshore Project Risk Analysis" Proceeding of Russian Arctic Offshore Conference, St. Petersburg, Russia, 1997.
7. Bercha, F.G., "Fault Trees for Everyday Risk Analysis", Proceedings of Canadian Society for Chemical Engineering, Risk Analysis Seminar, Edmonton, 1990.
8. Bercha, F.G., and Associates (Alberta) Limited, "Ice Scour Methodology Study", Final Report to Gulf Canada Resources, Calgary, AB, March 1986.
9. Bercha, F.G., "Application of Risk Analysis to Offshore Drilling and Risk Mitigation," Proceedings, Risk Analysis Seminar, Royal Commission of the Ocean Ranger Marine Disaster, Toronto, 1984.
10. Bercha, F.G., "Probabilities of Blowouts in the Canadian Arctic", North Sea Offshore Conference, Stavanger, Norway, 1978.
11. Bercha International Inc., "Alternative Oil Spill Occurrence Estimators for the Beaufort and Chukchi Seas – Fault Tree Method", Volumes I and II, OCS Study MMS 2002-047, Final Report to US Department of the Interior, Minerals Management Service, Alaska Outer Continental Shelf Region, August 2002.
12. Bercha International Inc., "Alternative Oil Spill Occurrence Estimators for their Variability for the Beaufort Sea – Fault Tree Method", Volumes I and II, OCS Study MMS 2005-O61, Final Report to US Department of the Interior, Minerals Management Service, Alaska Outer Continental Shelf Region, January 2006.
13. Brighton Webs Ltd., "BW D-Calc 1.0 Distribution Calculator", www.brighton-webs.co.uk/distributions/, 22 July 2005.
14. Doelp, L.C., G.K. Lee, R.E Linney, and R.W. Ormsby, "Quantitative Fault Tree Analysis: Gate-by-Gate Method", in Plant/Operations Progress, 4(3) 227-238, 1984.
15. Energy Resources Conservation Board of Alberta, "GASRISK – A Model to Estimate Risk to Public Safety for Uncontrolled Sour Gas Releases", Volume 6, April 1990.

16. E&P Forum, Quantitative Risk Assessment (QRA) Data Sheet Directory, The Oil Industry International Exploration and Production Forum, 25-28 Old Burlington Street, London, 1996.

17. Fairweather E&P Services, Inc., "Historical Blowout Study, North Slope, Alaska", Study for BP-Amoco Exploration (Alaska), Anchorage, AK, June 2000.

18. Fussell, J.B., "How to Hand Calculate System Reliability and Safety Characteristics", in IEEE Transactions on Reliability, R-24(3), 169-174, 1975.

19. Gadd, P.E., G. Hearon, C.B. Leidersdorf, W.G. McDougal, J. Ellsworth, and D. Thomas, "Slope Armor Design and Construction Northstar Production Island", in Proceedings, Volume 1, 16th International Conference on Port and Ocean Engineering under Arctic Conditions (POAC), Ottawa, ON, August 12-17, 2001.

20. Goff, R., J. Hammond, and A.C. Nogueira, "Northstar Sub Sea Pipeline Design of Metallurgy, Weldability, and Supporting Full Scale Bending Tests", in Proceedings, Volume 1, 16th International Conference on Port and Ocean Engineering under Arctic Conditions (POAC), Ottawa, ON, August 12-17, 2001.

21. Gulf Canada, "Analysis of Accidents in Offshore Operations Where Hydrocarbons Were Lost", Report by the Houston Technical Services Center of Gulf Research and Development Company for Gulf Canada Resources, Inc., Calgary, AB, 1981.

22. Hart Crowser Inc., "Estimation of Oil Spill Risk From Alaska North Slope, Trans-Alaskan Pipeline, and Arctic Canada Oil Spill Data Sets", OCS Study MMS 2000-007, Study for US Department of the Interior, Minerals Management Service, Alaska Outer Continental Shelf Region, Anchorage, AK, April 2000.

23. Henley, E.J., and H. Kumamoto, "Reliability Engineering and Risk Assessment", Printice-Hall, Englewood Cliffs, NJ, (ISBN 0-13-772251-6), 1981.

24. Hnatiuk, J., and K.D. Brown, "Sea Bottom Scouring in the Canadian Beaufort Sea", 9th Annual OTC, Houston, TX, May 2-5, 1983.

25. Holand, Per, Offshore Blowouts, Causes and Control, Gulf Publishing, Houston, Texas, USA, 1997.

26. Hoyland, A., and M. Rausand, "System Reliability Theory: Models and Statistical Methods", John Wiley and Sons, New York, NY, 1994.

27. Hunt, D.M., K.R. McClusky, R. Shirley, and R. Spitzenberger, "Facility Engineering for Arctic Conditions", in Proceedings, Volume 1, 16th International Conference on Port and Ocean Engineering under Arctic Conditions (POAC), Ottawa, ON, August 12-17, 2001.

28. ISO WG8, Arctic Structures, Reliability, Chapter 7, Section 7.2.2.3, October 30, 2006..

29. Lanan, G.A., and J.O. Ennis, "Northstar Offshore Arctic Pipeline Project", in Proceedings, Volume 1, 16th International Conference on Port and Ocean Engineering under Arctic Conditions (POAC), Ottawa, ON, August 12-17, 2001.

30. Leidersdorf, C.B., G.E. Hearon, R.C. Hollar, P.E. Gadd, and T.C. Sullivan, "Ice Gouge and Strudel Scour Data for the Northstar Pipelines", in Proceedings, Volume 1, 16th International Conference on Port and Ocean Engineering under Arctic Conditions (POAC), Ottawa, ON, August 12-17, 2001.

31. Lowrance, W.W., "Of Acceptable Risk", Kaufmann Inc., 1976.

32. Masterson, D.M., A.B. Christopherson, and J.W. Pickering, "Sheet Pile Design for Offshore Gravel Islands", in Proceedings, Volume 1, 16th International Conference on Port and Ocean Engineering under Arctic Conditions (POAC), Ottawa, ON, August 12-17, 2001.

33. Miller, D.L., "Hypersaline Permafrost under a Lagoon of the Arctic Ocean", in Proceedings, Volume 1, 16th International Conference on Port and Ocean Engineering under Arctic Conditions (POAC), Ottawa, ON, August 12-17, 2001.

34. MMS (Minerals Management Service), "Accidents Associated with Oil and Gas Operations: Outer Continental Shelf 1956-1990", OCS Report MMS 92-0058, 1992.

35. MMS (Minerals Management Service), "Federal Offshore Statistics: 1995. Leasing, exploration, production and revenues to December 31, 1995", US Department of the Interior, Mineral Management Service, Operations and Safety Management, OCS Report MMS 97-0007, 1997.

36. MMS (US Department of the Interior, Minerals Management Service, Alaska OCS Region), "Alaska Outer Continental Shelf - Beaufort Sea Planning Area Oil and Gas Lease Sale 144 - Final Environmental Impact Statement", Vol. II, OCS EIS/EA MMS 96-0012, May 1996.

37. MMS (US Department of the Interior, Minerals Management Service, Alaska OCS Region), "Alaska Outer Continental Shelf - Beaufort Sea Planning Area Oil and Gas Lease Sale 170 - Final Environmental Impact Statement", OCS EIS/EA MMS 98-0007, February 1998.

38. MMS (US Department of the Interior, Minerals Management Service, Alaska OCS Region), "Alaska Outer Continental Shelf - Chukchi Sea Oil & Gas Lease Sale 126 - Final Environmental Impact Statement", Vol. II, OCS EIS/EA MMS 90-0095, Anchorage, AK, January 1991.

39. MMS (US Department of the Interior, Minerals Management Service, Alaska OCS Region), "Undiscovered Oil and Gas Resources, Alaska Federal Offshore", OCS Monograph MMS 98-0054, Anchorage, AK, 1998.

40. MMS (US Department of the Interior, Minerals Management Service, Gulf of Mexico OCS Region), "Investigation of Shell Offshore Inc., Hobbit Pipeline Leak Ship Shoal Block 281, January 24, 1990, Gulf of Mexico, Offshore Louisiana", OCS Report MMS 91-0025, New Orleans, March 1991.

41. MMS (US Department of the Interior, Minerals Management Service, Gulf of Mexico OCS Region), "Investigation of the Exxon Company USA Pipeline Leak /Eugene Island Block 314, May 6, 1990, Gulf of Mexico, Offshore Louisiana", OCS Report MMS 91-0066, New Orleans, November 1991.

42. MMS (US Department of the Interior, Minerals Management Service, Gulf of Mexico OCS Regional Office), "Investigation of Chevron Pipe Line Company Pipeline Leak, South Pass Block 38, September 29, 1998, Gulf of Mexico Off the Louisiana Coast", OCS Report MMS 99-0053, New Orleans, September 1999.

43. MMS (US Department of the Interior, Minerals Management Service, Gulf of Mexico OCS Regional Office), "Investigation of Shell Offshore Inc., Hobbit Pipeline Leak, Ship Shoal Block 281, November 16, 1994, Gulf of Mexico, Off the Louisiana Coast", OCS Report MMS 97-0031, New Orleans, August 1997.

44. MMS (US Department of the Interior, Minerals Management Service, Gulf of Mexico OCS Regional Office), "Investigation of Shell Pipe Line Corporation Pipeline Leak South Pass Block 65 December 30, 1986, Gulf of Mexico off the Louisiana Coast", OCS Report MMS 87-0114, December 1987.

45. Modarres, M., M. Kaminsky, and V. Krisvtsov, "Reliability Engineering and Risk Analysis", Marcel Deker Inc., 1999.

46. O'Connor, M.J, and Associates Ltd., Preliminary Ice Keel/Seabed Interaction Study", Final Report to GCRI, March 1984.

47. Offshore Technology Research Center, "Comparative Risk Analysis for Deepwater Production Systems", Final Project Report for Minerals Management Service, January 2001.

48. OPL, "Field Development Concepts of the World", 1990.

49. Owen, L., D. Blanchet, and P. Flones, "The Northstar Project - Year-Round Production in the Alaskan Beaufort Sea", in Proceedings, Volume 1, 16th International Conference on Port and Ocean Engineering under Arctic Conditions (POAC), Ottawa, ON, August 12-17, 2001.

50. Paulin, M.J., D. Nixon, G.A. Lanan, and B. McShane, "Environmental Loadings & Geotechnical Considerations for the Northstar Offshore Pipelines", in Proceedings, Volume 1, 16th International Conference on Port and Ocean Engineering under Arctic Conditions (POAC), Ottawa, ON, August 12-17, 2001.

51. Roberts, N.H., W.E. Veseley, D.F. Haasl, and F.F. Goldberg, "Fault Tree Handbook", NUREG-0492, US Nuclear Regulatory Commission, Washington, DC, 1985.

52. S.L. Ross Environmental Research Ltd., "Blowout and Spill Probability Assessment for the Northstar and Liberty Oil Development Projects in the Alaska North Slope", Report to BP Exploration (Alaska), Inc., November 1998.

53. Ross, S.L., c.W. Ross, F. Lepine, and K.E. Langtry, "*Ixtoc I* Oil Blowout", Environment Canada E.P.S. Spill Technology Newsletter, pp. 245-256, July-August 1979.

54. S.L. Ross Environmental Research Ltd., "Blowout and Spill Probability Assessment for the Sable Offshore Energy Project", Report to Mobil Oil Canada Properties, November 1995.

55. S.L. Ross Environmental Research Ltd., "Contingency Plans to Monitor and Clean Up Large Spills from SOEP Offshore Facilities", Prepared for Sable Offshore Energy Project, Halifax, NS, March 31, 1998.

56. S.L. Ross Environmental Research Ltd., "Large Oil Spills and Blowouts from Exploration Drilling on Georges Bank: An Analysis of their Probability, Behaviour, Control and Environmental Effects", Chevron Canada Resources and Texaco Canada Petroleum Inc., submitted to the Georges Bank Review Panel, January 1999.

57. S.L. Ross Environmental Research Ltd., "Oil Spills Associated with the Terra Nova Development Project off Newfoundland: Risk Assessment; Spill Fate, Behaviour and Impact; Countermeasures; and Contingency Planning", Report to Petro-Canada Inc., December 1996.

58. S.L. Ross Environmental Research Ltd., "Panuke/Cohasset Field Development Project: Risk, Behaviour and Effects of Oil Spills", Report to IONA Resources Ltd. and Nova Scotia Resources Ltd., July 1989.

59. ScanPower A.S., "Blowout Frequency Assessment of Northstar", Report to BP Exploration (Alaska), Report No. 27.83.01/R1, Kjeller, Norway, July 2, 2001.

60. Sefton, A.D., "The Development of the U.K. Safety Case Regime: A Shift in Responsibility from Government to Industry", Offshore Technology Conference, Houston, USA, 1994.

61. Shared Services Drilling, "A Review of Alaska North Slope Blowouts, 1974-1997", June 30, 1998.

62. Sharples, B.P.M., J.J. Stiff, D.W. Kalinowski and W.G. Tidmarsh, "Statistical Risk Methodology: Application for Pollution Risks from Canadian Georges Bank Drilling Program", 21st Annual Offshore Technology Conference, Houston, TX, May 1-4, 1989.

63. Southwest Research Institute, "New Methods for Rapid Leak Detection in Offshore Pipelines", Final Report to Minerals management Service, US Department of the Interior, SwRI Project No. 04-4558, April 1992.

64. System Safety and Reliability Committee, Santa Barbara County, Energy Division, "Risk Matrix Guidelines", 1998.

65. U.S. Nuclear Regulatory Commission, "Reactor Safety Study", WASH-1400, NUREG-75/014, Appendix I – IV, October 1975.

66. Upstream Technology Group, "Analysis of Strudel Scours and Ice Gouges for the Liberty Development Pipeline", Final Draft, *no date.*

67. Weeks, W.F., P.W. Barnes, D.M. Rearic, and E. Reimnitz, "Some Probabilistic Aspects of Ice Gouging on the Alaskan Shelf of the Beaufort Sea", US Army Cold Regions Research and Engineering Laboratory, June 7, 1983.

68. Weeks, W.F., P.W. Barnes, D.M. Rearic, and E. Reimnitz, "Statistical Aspects of Ice Gouging on the Alaskan Shelf of the Beaufort Sea", US Army Cold Regions Research and Engineering Laboratory, 1982.

69. Wylie, W.W., and A.B. Visram, "Drilling Kick Statistics", Proceedings, IADC/SPE Drilling Conference, Houston, TX, February 27-March 2, 1980.

The Department of the Interior Mission

As the Nation's principal conservation agency, the Department of the Interior has responsibility for most of our nationally owned public lands and natural resources. This includes fostering sound use of our land and water resources; protecting our fish, wildlife, and biological diversity; preserving the environmental and cultural values of our national parks and historical places; and providing for the enjoyment of life through outdoor recreation. The Department assesses our energy and mineral resources and works to ensure that their development is in the best interests of all our people by encouraging stewardship and citizen participation in their care. The Department also has a major responsibility for American Indian reservation communities and for people who live in island territories under U.S. administration.

The Minerals Management Service Mission

As a bureau of the Department of the Interior, the Minerals Management Service's (MMS) primary responsibilities are to manage the mineral resources located on the Nation's Outer Continental Shelf (OCS), collect revenue from the Federal OCS and onshore Federal and Indian lands, and distribute those revenues.

Moreover, in working to meet its responsibilities, the **Offshore Minerals Management Program** administers the OCS competitive leasing program and oversees the safe and environmentally sound exploration and production of our Nation's offshore natural gas, oil and other mineral resources. The MMS **Royalty Management Program** meets its responsibilities by ensuring the efficient, timely and accurate collection and disbursement of revenue from mineral leasing and production due to Indian tribes and allottees, States and the U.S. Treasury.

The MMS strives to fulfill its responsibilities through the general guiding principles of: (1) being responsive to the public's concerns and interests by maintaining a dialogue with all potentially affected parties and (2) carrying out its programs with an emphasis on working to enhance the quality of life for all Americans by lending MMS assistance and expertise to economic development and environmental protection.

www.ingramcontent.com/pod-product-compliance
Lightning Source LLC
Chambersburg PA
CBHW082242310526
45795CB00013B/2010
9781514725580